Bridges of Mystery

Built by God...
To Span The Impossible

Sabra R. Bogart

PRESS

Bridges of Mystery
Built by God. . . To Span The Impossible
by Sabra R. Bogart

Printed in the United States of America

ISBN 9781629526553

www.xulonpress.com

Thank You

To my beloved husband, Guy. . .for his steady strength and sound counsel that helped my family re-focus after the storm. We all love him deeply and look forward to his fun and laughter when we see him again.

To my beautiful daughters, Dana, Christi, and Lezlie who have always been an inspiration and a joy to my heart. I could not have made it through some of the difficult years without their love and support.

To my "special friends," Sandra and Mike Hussie whose caring friendship and love made the "way" across some of the rugged bridges seem a little less treacherous.

A special "thank you" to those who took the time to read and critique portions of this book. The list is long, but I especially thank Chuck and Jelayne Jorgenson, who in the very beginning of these pages gave me thoughtful and strong incentive to continue.

My special thanks to Sally E. Stuart, author of Christian Writers' Market Guide, for her valuable and "down to earth" suggestions and encouragement in the evaluation of my 2009 book proposal that helped me stay focused on the "finish line".

The picture on this page was created by my grandson, Adam Joseph Kane, especially for the cover of this book. He is a student at Western Washington University, studying English and working toward a career in Creative Writing. His artwork skillfully depicts some of the allegories of bridges presented at the beginning of each chapter.

Introduction

There are many bridges that we must cross in our lives, some of them are strong and inviting, and some are old and creaky with loose planks and treacherous surprises. These bridges are filled with mystery and wonder and are designed by the Master Builder Himself to lead the traveler on a journey of discovery into the magnificent and unique design that He has for each of us. However, the most wonderful truth that we discover as we approach each new bridge is that **we are never expected to cross it alone**.

I have had many opportunities to share my life's story with women and teens from all walks of life and I am always eager to seek out every opportunity to share the hope that my Savior has placed in my heart. I believe that my experiences will encourage and prepare others in this journey, in much the same way that other travelers stopped to help me along some of the most treacherous parts of my journey.

In 1964 I chanced upon a beautiful poem that inspired my heart. From that moment on, I wanted to be used by the Master to build bridges for others that travel after me.

I copied the poem in my notes and frequently opened the yellowed pages over the years to remember the wonderful quest that God placed in my heart so many years ago.

"Building The Bridge"

A pilgrim, going a lone highway
Came at evening, cold and gray
To a chasm, deep and vast and wide.
The old man crossed in the twilight dim.
The chasm held no fears for him
But he paused when he reached the other side
And built a bridge to span the tide.
"Old man," said a fellow pilgrim near,
"Why waste your time in building here?
Your journey ends with the close of day
You never again will pass this way.
You've crossed the chasm deep and wide
Why build ye here at eventide?"
The pilgrim raised his old gray head,
"My friend, in the path I've come," he said,
"There followeth after me today
A fair haired youth who must pass this way.
The chasm which held no fears for me
To the fair haired youth may a pitfall be.
He, too, must cross in the twilight dim.
My friend, I am building this bridge for him."
                              —by Will Dromgoole[1]

I pray that this book will become a bridge of hope in lives that often struggle against the hopeless echo of the word, *impossible*. My heart's desire has always been to build bridges that will help others cross the most treacherous rivers and chasms of life.

God's life giving forgiveness and grace; His persistent and restorative healing; the compelling promise of His eternal presence, and the magnificence of His "Father's love;" have kept and nurtured His plan

---

[1] "Building The Bridge," by William Dromgoole. Search for Copyright conducted by Thomson & Thomson, 1750 K St. NW, Suite 200, Washington, DC 20006-2305. Search No.: 103940411. July 28, 2003. Research of the registration/renewal files of the Copyright Office failed to reveal registration in connection with the poem, BUILDING THE BRIDGE by William R. Dromgoole.

in my life until I can do no less than turn and offer it freely to anyone who may travel these same bridges after me.

The clouds on the horizon are thickening and the way that was once clear and open has now become narrow and hidden by the threat of false promises and conflicting solutions. However, amid the shadows and storm clouds brewing in the distance, God's truth and crystal promises of hope and life still offer *a bridge across the most treacherous waters*.

Sabra Bogart

Contents

❧ 1 ❧

"The Billy Goats Gruff Bridge"
— The Bridge of Rejection —

— Allegory —

Beautiful pastures in the distance beckon to the heart with soft and gentle sounds of happiness and freedom just beyond the bridge. If only there was some other way around such a terrifying crossing.

The rickety old bridge, prematurely weathered by the onslaught of many struggles and cares, has left protruding nails and loose boards that rattle and clatter beneath each halting step. Splintered railings hang from the battered posts as though tempting unsuspecting travelers to grasp their rotting supports. To trip and lose your footing here could cause you to plunge through one of the treacherous spaces to the murky depths below. The first inclination is to avoid this bridge, but the beautiful pastures in the distance seem to call to the heart with promise and hope for anyone willing to risk everything to cross.

To further threaten this crossing an evil troll can be seen emerging from the shadows below. His loud shrieking threats of failure pierce the darkness from beneath the bridge, warning all who dare attempt this crossing to retreat to the barren wasteland or risk sure destruction.

Tears of hopelessness sting your cheeks as you turn once again to the emptiness that surrounds the lonely landscape on this side of the bridge. The loud and constant threats from beneath the bridge now drive you deeper and deeper into the darkness.

"The Billy Goat's Gruff Bridge"
—The Bridge of Rejection—

I could feel the challenging gaze of the young woman standing in the shadows at the back of the room. As I glanced in her direction she seemed to move further into the shadows of the alcove, and I wondered if she would still be there when I finished talking with the women and teenage girls that had gathered at the front of the auditorium to speak with me. I could not help but watch for her out of the corner of my vision, and whispered a silent prayer for God to keep her from leaving.

As soon as I could free myself from the others, I made my way to the back of the room and found her leaning against the wall in the shadows. I could feel the angry challenge in her eyes as I approached her and my heart was broken with compassion for her. Her words pierced the space between us as I whispered a prayer in my spirit for God to give me His words and His heart for her.

"You'd better not be lyin' to me!" she demanded.

"Lying about what?" I asked, fearful that the wrong response would cause her to bolt and run.

"You'd better be tellin' me the truth about Jesus Christ—that He really can 'come in' and make me whole again!"

"I have staked my whole life on that!" I said "And if He did it for me, He will do it for you."

She turned and ran from the room.

For the past hour I had shared God's miracle-working love that had taken my broken and shattered life and transformed it into one of wholeness, purpose and joy through the saving grace of Jesus Christ. I told of God's love that sent His Son from heaven to heal and restore lives like mine that the world had discarded as unwanted and hopeless. I could sense God's love in the room as He touched and ministered to the women and teens that had sat motionless for the past hour while I shared the story of my life. The annual Mother/Daughter Banquet had attracted mothers and daughters from a wide spectrum of farmers and ranchers along this eastern plains community.

The pastor's wife told me the tragic story of the devastating events that happened in the girl's life. She had suffered unspeakable trauma within her family that had resulted in a broken life for her and other members of her family. The pastor of the little church and his wife

17

had taken her into their home and had sought counseling for her with a specialist in a large city. After the last visit, the doctor had expressed to them that the girl was so deeply damaged that he could not do any more for her. He felt that the girl's life was destroyed beyond repair. His prognosis: "No hope!"

I spent many nights laying awake, wondering about her life and praying for her.

Had she met Jesus that night?

Had she experienced the incredible freedom of His forgiveness that would wrap her in a cloak of cleanness and purity and then offer her spotless before the throne of the Father?

Had she come to know the amazing power of His love that could release those that had harmed her in forgiveness at the foot of the cross?

Had she been able to forgive herself amidst the accusations and whispers of an unthinking and unforgiving world?

I never heard what happened with her life, but I do know that God, in His tender love, brought her to that little church that night. The pastor's wife assured me that she would carefully follow-up with her.

Only Jesus can heal the pain and broken spirit that has been shattered by such a devastating experience. Her emotions had been stretched and broken like a rubber band extended beyond the limits of endurance. Her future had been stolen and the world had condemned her to the place of shattered lives—as "un-fixable." When we try within our own finite minds to figure out a solution for one so devastated, we throw up our hands and shake our heads like the specialist that declared her as lost and hopeless.

Our beloved Savior looked down through the ages and saw her in her broken and shattered life and came to die and rise again—to give her—a brand new life "in Him".

Perhaps someone read the old fairy tale, "The Billy Goats Gruff Bridge," to me as a small child, but I remember thinking how terrible it would be to have to go over such a scary bridge with an awful troll living underneath. Now, as I think of the many bridges that I have crossed in my life, I think that I may have spent most of my childhood struggling to avoid the scary troll living beneath the "Billy Goats Gruff Bridge."

This bridge is erected in our lives by the painful circumstances of life. It seems endless in its span and the loud threats of failure coming from the shadows beneath the bridge produce fear of the darkness beneath and certain destruction for one who might attempt to cross alone.

The very early years of my life seem almost like memories from a fairy tale. My daddy raised cotton in the rich farmland of the Mississippi delta. During the hard times when we must have been very poor, we lived in an old weathered house built high off the ground to withstand the threat of rising water along the banks of the bayou. I can still see my daddy sitting in the wooden chair tilted on two legs against the kitchen wall waiting for mother to finish cooking his supper, and the warm smells of cornbread coming from the stove.

There were other times when things must have been good and we lived in a different house away from the bayou. I have wonderful memories in this house of the people who worked for us; people who seemed more like members of the family rather than workers around the house. During those times my daddy seemed like a king who ruled his own empire.

Garfield was a slender black man with sort of sad, kind eyes who was a trusted friend to my mother and to us children. I remember the day that mother sat the three of us down and told us that we could always trust Garfield with our very lives, like there was some secret threat that we were too young to understand. From that day on, Garfield always seemed to be nearby, watching over us wherever we went. We understood that his authority was law, and to sass him, was the same as sassing mother! Respect for authority was a cardinal rule for any well-brought-up child, regardless of social or financial status, and to sass an adult authority figure was a fate far worse than certain death!

There was the cook, Dolly who was small, but whose sharp reprimand would strike fear in the heart of my brothers and me if we ventured into that sacred domain while she was cooking. I remember the stacks of wonderful warm pancakes with the butter drizzled down the sides, that she would have waiting for us in the kitchen for breakfast, and the endless squabble between my brothers over who could eat the most. She was small and bossy, but she ruled over the kitchen with complete authority. I remember the day that my brothers and I exploded in laughter as we watched her chase Garfield from the kitchen with the big iron skillet.

These, and others, were wonderful happy times that were etched indelibly into my small child's heart. I have often wondered what special ingredient triggers a strong memory in the heart of a child. I think that it must be some unusually wonderful sense of exposure that causes the memory to want to take a snapshot to be recorded forever in the scrapbook of the heart. I think that the frightening and fearful memories are recorded there, as well, but there seems to be some protective instinct built into us that chooses not to save some of those snapshots, or, at least to hide them in a very remote place until the heart is stronger.

There are many memories of special times that I spent with my father. I accompanied him at times on his daily inspection of the rich furrows that spread out before him on his cotton farms. I remember the way he would squat between the rows of just-planted seeds, resting one hip on the back of his heel as he reached down for a handful of the dark rich earth. I can still see him as he would mash it between his thumb and fingers then draw it to his nose as if measuring the content of moisture by the scent of the black soil. Then he would push his hat back on his head with his forefinger while tilting his head to the sky to inspect the appearance of clouds on the horizon.

I remember the excitement of watching hired men and women flood his fields with their long canvas sacks when it was time to pick the rows and rows of white cotton bursting from the hip high plants that he had planted months earlier. As the plants matured, the seed-pods would dry and open, revealing their rich treasure of cotton that looked to me, like snow-white ice cream spilling out of a cone. The sharp points on the cotton bolls, when dried, were like knives that would rip and tear at the workers hands, leaving them bleeding and raw by evening. I remember my glee the day daddy gave me a whole quarter as payment for the cotton I gingerly picked and stuffed into a small paper sack.

I especially loved to go with him to the little country store where other farmers gathered to discuss the prospects of their crops and the threat of the land being too wet or too dry for newly planted seed. He would always give me a nickel for candy and we would share an ice cold Coca-Cola from a bottle stuffed with salty peanuts. I remember the day that the little black boy with his tattered overalls and bare feet ventured into the center of the store and began to dance in perfect timing to some imaginary music that played from within his own soul. His big dark eyes shone with expectation as the men began to clap with laughter from their wooden chairs tilted against the old wooden boards that lined the walls. The boys grin broke into laughter as the men began to toss pennies at his feet. I also remember, but never quite understood, the sad feeling that I had in my stomach as I watched him gather the pennies into his small hands and run out the door.

I remember sitting on the front steps of our house each afternoon waiting for daddy to arrive home from work, and I always ran squealing with joy to greet him at the end of the day.

Even though we now lived in town, there was a bayou that ran down the center of our street with homes on both sides. A hanging wooden footbridge crossed to the other side of the street close to our house, but I was always afraid to cross because of the smell of the ugly green contents that seeped through the cattails beneath. On my first day of kindergarten my big brother, Brooks, lifted me sidesaddle to ride on the cross bar of his bicycle across the rickety old bridge. My fears of the ugly swamp beneath the bridge gave way to pride as my brother reassured me that he would take care of me.

I also remember the morning my mother dressed my brothers, and me and put us in a car to go and live with my aunt. My life was changed abruptly with this event and the happy years dissolved like smoke in the wake of the angry separation and divorce that followed. I am sure that my mom must have offered some explanation about our hurried departure, but I do not remember being concerned or aware that this was to be the end of my life together with my daddy. In later years my oldest brother told me that he knew why we were leaving that day. He was nine years old and seemed to feel, even then, a great deal of anger toward daddy. Perhaps mother had taken him into her confidence concerning the circumstances of our departure, or perhaps he was old enough to observe the unhappiness that must have existed between them.

Life was forever changed for me that day as we left our little house in Mississippi. Those happy memories of childhood would soon fade with the clouds of confusion that occupied my thoughts and shattered my young life.

The precious security that comes from knowing that you have two parents who love you was gone forever. There were no answers for a child of five. My mother was bitter and changed, and I felt the desperate pain that she suffered because my daddy had forsaken us for someone else. As a child I was torn between sympathy for my mother and protection for my daddy against mother's anger. From that day on, I was alone. My two brothers were there, but the nurture and

21

support that can come only through the careful attention of parents had disappeared.

This was the early 1940's and there were very few jobs for women, especially for ones with only a high school education. Mother struggled with the task of raising three young children alone and without the benefit of child support. She worked for practically pennies during the day and attended business school at night. Greenville, Mississippi was a very small town and we were able to walk to and from school. After school, I was left in the care and supervision of my older brothers until mother returned home in the evening.

These were sad days for all of us. Mother had become consumed with survival and bitterness, while my daddy was consumed with his new life. My oldest brother, who was only nine years old, was expected to assume responsibilities for the watchful care of my brother, William and me. A heavy burden, indeed, for one so young. Mother's frustration often exploded in anger toward him. His young shoulders were burdened far beyond his years and he began to withdraw from her into his own shell. I spent much of my time silently defending him in my heart for I loved him deeply.

My middle brother was my hero. We all had our childhood stolen, but William always seemed to have his own little world under control. His philosophies of life, even at seven, captivated me and seemed to somehow make life reasonable in the middle of the turmoil.

My heart ached to be accepted by the other little girls in school. There were stories of wonderful birthday parties with colorful party favors and balloons. Mother was never home until late, and my brothers were always occupied with exploits of their own, so one day, I decided to plan a birthday party of my own. I don't think I knew or cared when my birthday was supposed to be. After inviting some of the other girls in my second grade class with homemade invitations; I walked down to the local dime store and shoplifted all of the pretty things that I would need to please my guests. There were little red plastic whistles and beautiful balloons that I secretly stuffed into my dress. On the day of the party, I pulled a chair up to the kitchen counter and made delicious peanut butter and jelly sandwiches for my guests. It still amazes me to remember that some little girls actually came that afternoon to my party. My heart was thrilled with the joy of acceptance that I felt from their attendance.

My heart grows sad at this painful memory. I see all around me in the world today, children with the same sadness in their eyes because they, too, are struggling to cross this Billy Goats Gruff Bridge. The terrible troll shouts from the darkness beneath the bridge that they will never make it to the other side. They will never taste the sweetness of the pasture on the other side of the bridge where the soul's hunger for love and acceptance are satisfied. We live in a society today where hundreds of thousands of children are thrust into the same circumstances of growing up alone in a world that even adults find difficult and sometimes impossible to navigate.

Divorce in those days was rare and carried with it a heavy stigma of guilt and failure. I shall never forget the day that my mother took me with her for a court appearance where she desperately sought child support. As I sat in the cold and somber chambers that day, I remember the face of the angry judge as he addressed my mother. The accusing sting of his eyes seemed to wield an angry whip that ripped at my mother's countenance. Society's stern judgment of a woman weak enough to dissolve her marriage for any reason, even infidelity, was crystal clear. Her shoulders sank with the burden of guilt and shame lavished on her by the image of authority behind the great wooden desk. A sense of shame and embarrassment swept over me, as well. All hope seemed to fade from mother's heart. Society offered little understanding or forgiveness for one who was willing to venture into such deep waters.

— **Broken Tomorrows** —

Finally, when I was 10 years old, my mom realized that she could no longer leave us at home alone to fend for ourselves. We had basically become what the world today would call street children. We were the kids down the street that you would not want your children playing with. My brother had stolen a watch from a neighbor and I remember the terror and despair in Mother's voice as she screamed at him from the next room. What was to become of us all? We lived as paupers and she saw no way out. She was faced with a hopeless future and frightened for our welfare. She finally allowed my dad to take my two brothers to live with him on his farm. After vowing that he would never have me, she began searching for an inexpensive boarding school that would take a ten year old girl.

23

There were hushed conversations between my mother and one of my aunts as they discussed the two different schools that were possibilities. Their voices were always quickly extinguished when I entered the room of the tiny old motel where we were now living. Mother finally decided on a school in the small Mississippi town of French Camp located on the famous Natchez Trace.

There is so much about the Christian life that even after so many years of knowing, trusting and leaning on Him that I still do not understand. Someone has said, "hindsight is always 20-20." I would prefer to say "God-sight is crystal clear!" We usually do not see what God is doing in our lives until many years later. I know now that God was deeply involved in my mother's choice to place me in that particular school, even though she was still many years away from knowing Jesus Christ as her Savior. The Bible says in Psalm 139:16, *"Your eyes saw my substance, being yet unformed and in Your book they all were written, The days fashioned for me, When as yet there were none of them."*

The skies were gray and dreary as we arrived at the school that September morning in 1946. The constant downpour of rain had made the yard around the three-story old brick administration building almost impassable with mud. French Camp Academy had never taken students under high school age before, but for some reason they agreed to take me on a trial basis. After spending a long time in the school president's office where he and my mother talked of many things that I did not understand we were taken next door to the girl's dormitory. This building, similar in appearance, stood like a twin sister next to the one that we had just left. We climbed the steep wooden stairway leading to the second floor entrance to the girl's dormitory, anxious to get out of the downpour of rain that pelted us as we made our way across the muddy campus. The first floor of the old building, built in 1929, was the school dining hall and kitchen. As we entered the second floor, I remember being the center of attention with all of the older girls in the "big girl's dormitory."

The drab room that was to be my new home had high ceilings covered with faded tin that had once been ornately decorated in squares. Beneath the large windows with their stained and yellowing shades, stood the old silver radiators that coughed and banged loudly as the steam from the boiler below filled their pipes. Small single beds with wire springs supported mattresses covered with faded blue ticking,

24

soiled and worn thin from years of frequent juvenile occupants. The floors creaked loudly beneath our feet with each step. I would soon learn to know each dark, oiled board with its own personal noise so well that I could easily steal down the dark halls late at night for secret meetings with the other girls. Water spots soiled the ceiling and walls as reminders of the constant rain that assaulted this new and empty world. The old plaster walls, once grand in appearance, were now cracked and peeling from many layers of carelessly applied paint.

In a corner of my room mother placed the new metal footlocker with the shiny padlock that she had been instructed to provide for me. Within the footlocker were sheets and towels on which she had carefully sewn my name. The day she had taken me shopping for school clothes to take to my new school, was one of the happiest days that I can remember. We were like schoolgirls planning for the big dance. I remember the ecstasy of trying on the beautiful plaid gingham dresses with their little ribbons and bows. Mother allowed me to choose five for my very own. They had all been neatly folded, along with crisp, new pajamas and other necessary items, which she placed into the footlocker along with a hairbrush and new saddle oxford shoes for school. Knowledge of the treasures waiting for me within the shiny footlocker served to postpone any awareness of what was really happening in my life. I could not wait to open it to touch all of the beautiful things that were mine. I could not remember personally owning these things before, and as I looked inside the little footlocker I thought that I was very rich, indeed. It now contained my whole life.

Mother had placed in a corner of the little footlocker a picture of herself in a silver metal frame that had always rested on her dresser in the small one room apartment that we had occupied together. In the lonely years to follow, this picture was to become a lighthouse in my heart, offering the promise of safety and hope amid the crashing winds of loneliness and despair that relentlessly pounded away at my spirit. Even in the darkness of my room at night, I could reach out and touch the metal frame and be momentarily comforted by mother's imaginary presence.

In my heart that day, as a 10 year old girl, I never even imagined the course of my future from that day on. After having raised three daughters of my own, I think that it might be a rare thing, indeed, for any 10 year old child to even consider what effect today's decisions might have on all of the tomorrow's yet to be. Perhaps my mother had considered the consequences that such a separation might mean for her, but I don't think she dared consider the impact that her choices might have on my life. I am sure that she told herself that she was doing the best thing for me. Very soon after leaving me at the school that day, she embarked on a new marriage. Even though I visited at Christmas and a short time in the summers, I never felt a part of her life from that time on. There were other marriages beyond that one that would not include me. Now my real memories of a family seemed to be built around a fading past relationship with my elderly grandparents who had always seemed to love me in a special way.

I often felt over the years, a deep sadness in my heart for the little 10-year-old tucked away in my memories. She would never again experience the warm embrace of a mother's arms to soothe the hurt of a skinned knee, or hear the comforting sound of her reassuring voice in the middle of the night to chase away the fears of the dark. There would be no one to wipe away the tears imposed by the heartache of careless words spoken in anger by others.

A few years ago, I was speaking for a women's retreat in Loveland, Colorado, and as was my custom, I shared the story of my life at the end of our time together. Many women stopped by to talk to me afterwards, but one woman leaned forward and whispered softly in my ear, "I love that little 10 year old girl!" In another moment, she was gone. There are times in our walk with God, when something that seems so ordinary in the telling is difficult to convey to others. In that instant, I felt like I had just heard a whisper from God to my spirit—a healing declaration from heaven! I sat there transfixed as I tried to hide my tears. Somehow, I knew that my Father in heaven wanted to remind me that the little girl in those terrible dark years had never really been alone. He was there, and He had loved me, even then. He was there the night I screamed out with fear from the terrible nightmares and delirium that accompanied the red measles. He was there the day that I sat alone in my room rocking and sobbing because I did not have 25¢ to pay the women who came in their wagon to pick up our laundry on Fridays and deliver it clean and ironed on Mondays. He was there through the long relentless rains that swept the drab campus in the winter and kept us prisoners in a sea of mud and dampness. He was there through the long and lonely nights, as I lay awake—afraid to move in the darkness.

Hopefully, the day will come for each of us to see and understand the truth of His involvement in the design of our lives for His great purpose. Psalm 139:17 says, *"How precious are your thoughts about me, O God! They are innumerable!"* (NLT) We may not understand these powerful words from God's Word when we are in the middle of such a deep heartache, but they are true.

It still amazes me that we can live and walk and trust for a lifetime, but still need a loving touch from the Master to heal tender places in our spirit that we had considered years ago to be whole.

After my mom left me at the school that day, several of the older girls took me under their wing. They showed me their rooms, brushed and combed the long tangle of hair that cascaded down my back, and asked me many questions about my family. I remember saying things to them that day to impress them—to reassure them, and perhaps myself, that there really were those who cared deeply about me. I made my first attempt to fantasize about a fictitious world that hated to give me up. I am still amazed at my young heart's need to convince them and me that someone really did love me.

That first year at the school was filled with many surprises for me. There were so many desperate situations among the older girls that I struggled to understand. Their lives were filled with sad and amazing stories of the pain that they had endured before coming to the school; pain that had ripped at their hearts and left empty, lonely shells. In the late hours, huddled beneath blankets with flashlights in different rooms, I would hear whispered tales of both physical and emotional abuse from those of trust in their lives. Sometimes sandwiched in between stories of their past, someone would begin to share bits and pieces of stolen encounters with one of the older boys living in the large building with white columns up on the hill. "The hill" was the boy's dormitory and there were many stories of their raucous behavior that circulated throughout the girl's dorm. Any news of a new incident on "the hill" sent shock waves of excitement throughout the hot line of gossip behind closed doors. Their stories often frightened and shocked me. After tiptoeing back to my own room after one of the secret gatherings, I would lay awake, my heart pounding, with many terrible and exciting, bits of information. Even though I was only 10, I loved being included in their late night sessions. I think that they loved to watch my face for the expressions of shock and wonder that would sweep over me with their juicy tales of worldly behavior. These dangerous late night encounters gave me a fearful sense of belonging to a kind of secret society.

On Sundays we were required to march single file to the local church in town for Sunday school and church. The old wooden church with its weathered steeple stood as a proud anchor for the town's people. The local men and women were gracious and friendly to us, but always seemed to keep their distance as we filed into the pews. In the years to come, I would learn to love and appreciate this tiny little town of French Camp, Mississippi, with its farmers and proprietors of the few small stores and the local gas station.

When we attended church on Sundays, the boys from the school were required to sit on one side of the church and the girls on the other. We were not allowed to speak during our march to church or during the service or we would receive demerits. A demerit meant the assigned punishment of an hour's work. These demerits were handed out like lollipops by angry and distraught staff in a never-ending effort to maintain some sort of order. For some of us, our disruptive behavior in church meant hours of work later, but always a badge of acceptance by our peers.

Every night, Miss Kaiser, the housemother of the girl's dormitory, would walk the halls at precisely 10 pm while shaking her large silver bell with the wooden handle up and down for "lights out." Miss Kaiser was a tall stern woman with eyes that seemed to pierce the darkness that filled the hallways after dark like a laser that scanned around corners and through walls. She had a jaw that was set like steel against the threat of disobedience from anyone who dared question her authority. I can still hear the sharp cadence of her heels as her black laced shoes clipped the old boards in the hallways on her rounds. At the sound of her bell, girls would scurry through the halls to complete their necessities before the repeat bell five minutes later. Any infraction beyond this point would incur Miss Kaiser's sure and instant wrath. Her sharp words would pierce my empty young heart with terror and I would run for the safety of my room and the closed door that would shelter me from her stern look. I always hurried to climb into my bunk before the empty darkness would close in around me and crush me with its fearful heaviness. The silent emptiness was only broken by the sound of the rats running around in the ceiling overhead or the loud moaning and clanging from the old radiators under the windows. Then I would pull my pillow tight about my face so that no one else could hear me and I would cry myself to sleep in complete loneliness and heartache.

Every night I would whisper a prayer into my pillow in the dark, *"Dear God, someday—somehow, please give me a home and a family again! Just give me someone to love me."*

I didn't know who God was. God was just someone out there, somewhere that you ask for the impossible! How could the great God who created the universe care about a lonely, bedraggled little girl in a broken down boarding school in Mississippi? The world did not want me, why would God, if there was a God. But, you see, I had no one else to ask. **I would learn years later that the great God of the impossible had heard my childhood cry.**

The second year that I was there, the school decided to take a small brick building down the hill from the girl's dormitory and open a home for little girls. The elderly housemother of the new little girl's dormitory was a small frail woman with wire framed glasses that sat on the end of her nose as she spoke. Her eyes were stern and challenging and her manner seemed guarded, as though hiding some deep pain of her own. She also wore the black lace shoes with the big heels that clicked through the halls in the night. She called me into her room one day and told me that there would be a new girl arriving that had a handicap. She told me that she was to be placed in the room with me and I would be expected to help her as much as possible.

This was my first encounter with anyone who was handicapped in such a way, and I was immediately struck with the burden of this new responsibility. Ann was a Down's syndrome child, somewhere around the age of 10 or 11. Her mother and father were very gentle and kind people that talked to me as if I was an adult that had agreed to walk on water, in their stead. I could surely see that Ann was different, but did not yet understand the heavy responsibility that being her constant overseer would mean throughout the coming year. At first, she seemed shy and withdrawn, but I would soon learn that she was very strong willed and easily agitated. Her explosive anger and unusual strength frightened me and my efforts to calm her were often inadequate. I felt responsibility toward her, but there were times when I was frightened by her angry outbursts. I still wonder why God placed her in my life. Perhaps it was to teach me His love and mercy toward one of His "special lambs". I would add patience, but I know that He is still working on that one, even now.

Over the span of years that I spent at the school, there were quite a few girls with severe physical handicaps. The one that I loved the most was Ramona, a victim of palsy, whose face and eyes shone like the sun when she talked. Her red wavy hair glistened in the sunlight with each toss of her head as she would struggle to form words to speak. I can still see the beauty of her countenance as she laughed out loud each time she saw me walking toward her in the halls. Her body writhed and jerked with each of her steps, but the sparkle in her eyes made it impossible to focus on her handicap. I loved her the first moment I met her and I am still not sure that she was not one of God's special angels (Heb. 13:2), sent to brighten my drab little corner and encourage my heart. I sometimes wonder how long the heart of God could stand to be without her beautiful sparkling laughter around His throne. I look forward to seeing her there, and know that heaven will be a more beautiful place because of her presence.

It was during the time that I was living in the little girl's dormitory that an elderly woman from the town came to our dorm one day and asked the housemother for permission to begin a Bible memory program with us. She offered prizes each week for anyone completing the assigned memorization of a weekly chapter in the gospel of John. The possibility of winning the prizes was tempting to me, for I owned nothing. I worked very hard to memorize the long chapters from the little booklet she had given me and was faithfully rewarded each week with a wonderful prize.

The first one was a small plastic cross that absorbed light from my window during the day and then glowed brilliantly all night from its place on the windowsill. How I loved that little cross. It warmed my heart like a special friend that seemed to watch over me in the dark hours of the night. I still treasure it deeply along with the small copy of Pilgrim's Progress that I won the next week. After many weeks of hard work, the sweet lady awarded me a beautiful new King James Version of the Bible for memorizing all of the chapters contained in the booklet. In the front of it she pasted a certificate of accomplishment with my name inscribed. That wonderful old tattered Bible with its now torn and yellowed pages became an anchor of truth in my life. I often thank God for the sweet little lady who had the vision to find a way to place God's Word in the heart of a little girl she did not even know. As I look back over those years, I see the hand of God working in my life in a very real way. Those chapters in the gospel of John would become foundation stones in my life—more precious than any possessions I could ever own in the years to come.

One warm Sunday afternoon upon returning to the dorm after lunch, I sat on the floor in the small sitting room playing checkers with some of the girls. The conversation soon shifted to the often common pastime of speculating on what I call the "someday syndrome".

"Someday, I'm going to be. . ." or, "someday, I will go. . ." or more importantly, "someday, when my mother comes to take me home. . ."

The housemother was sitting in a chair nearby doing some sewing and listening to our chatter. She finally interrupted our rounds of "one-up-man-ship" with a sharp, impatient declaration that would strike my heart like a spear and sever all the threads of hope to which I clung.

"Listen to me, girls!" she said sharply "The only reason you are at French Camp Academy today is because there is no one in the whole world that cares anything about you. The sooner you get that straight, the better off you will be!"

I am sure today that she honestly thought that she was doing us a favor. Perhaps she sought to save us from further disillusionment about the reality of our circumstances. Whatever her reasons, we all sat in stunned silence for what seemed like an eternity.

I remember as an adult, hearing a psychologist on television talk about the prisoners of war in Vietnam. He stated that even though the enemy may place a prisoner in isolation in the deepest, darkest pit in the most remote part of the world—if that prisoner knows that there is someone, somewhere that cares for him, he **can** survive. But, if the enemy can convince him that there is no one in the whole world that cares anything about him, he cannot survive!

That housemother, in one short statement, shattered all of the hopes and dreams of my young heart. From that day on, I became as hopeless, angry, and bitter as the older girls were. I learned that, regardless of age or circumstances in all of our lives, we had at least one thing in common—we were all outcasts. **We were all kids that no one else wanted!** Most of the girls, like myself, were either products of broken homes, or disciplinary problems—some of them just one step short of the reform school.

When I entered the eighth grade, I moved back into the older girl's dormitory. The education that I acquired from the other girls soon began to shape my personality with resentment and rebellion toward those in authority around me. The pain of rejection by my mother and the world became so intense that like the other girls; I learned to protect myself by building an impenetrable wall around my heart to protect me from those that might hurt me. How could I ever trust myself to be vulnerable to anyone again? My attitude toward others became harsh and angry, daring anyone to approach me.

The reality of my attitude hit me squarely in the face one day when a member of the staff stopped me in one of the hallways. She had questioned me about something and I responded with my usual curt reply.

"You have the nastiest disposition of anyone I have ever known!" was her angry retort.

I turned on my heels, reeling from the verbalized statement that penetrated my safe little haven of protection, and ran trembling with remorse from the building. I ran across the short distance between the two buildings and threw myself on my bed, sobbing with shame. I wanted to hide forever from the ugliness that dared to view my secret pain. This person's words had invaded what I thought was a fortified place of protection, a place of retreat beyond my wall that the world could not reach. I did not know how to be acceptable to her or this world that did not need or want me. In the reality of such stinging criticism, my wall had dissolved and left me exposed to the world! The awful thing about living in such fearful isolation is that you are afraid to allow yourself to be touched or approached by others; yet at the same time, you are desperate for someone to reach beyond the wall and soothe the confused hurt and make it end.

Was there anyone in the entire world that could possibly care enough to penetrate the lonely isolation in my life? My world had become desolate and empty. A deep loneliness engulfed my heart and caused me to become very self-sufficient and independent. I thought that I would no longer need or trust anyone! This loneliness was not for the company of other people around me, because the other girls were always close by. No, this loneliness was the aching emptiness of knowing that you do not belong to anyone. This kind of loneliness tears at the heart and destroys the soul. The troll living in the darkness beneath the bridge had won. Crossing the bridge to the beautiful green fields beyond was now impossible.

The years passed slowly and painfully. Trouble among the students and staff was very common. We were kids always looking for extremes in our world because even extreme situations of discipline broke the monotony of the endless days of sameness. The school went from bad to worse. The students were angry and bitter, bound together with one common cause, to break the rules.

There seemed to be a complete lack of caring, purpose and professionalism among the teachers and staff. Gossip and rumors plagued their lives and often filtered down to the students. There was an absence of respect for them from us, or among themselves for each other. We tested them at every turn by pushing, prodding and antagonizing them every moment of each day. I did not know why then, but now I know that we were longing for someone that could stand the test—someone that would not break under our pressure. We were searching for a standard of integrity and strength; a glimmer of light that would not waver in the darkness of our world. There were many loud accusations, demands and threats toward us concerning wrong behavior, but we felt that not one of them had the strength or caring to look us in the eye and stand for something! There was no real right and wrong—there was only wrong! We knew we were wrong—but where would we find a measuring stick—a standard of trust to live by? We needed someone in which to believe! We struck out at the wishy-washy weakness that we saw in every person of authority that confronted our broken world. We did not understand our reactions to the school staff at the time, but I learned later that most of our hostility towards those in authority over us was basically rooted in a lack of respect. We were looking for an impossible dream in a dark world.

As we ate dinner in the dining hall one night nearing the end of my eighth grade, a member of the staff stood and announced that the school had reached a financial crisis. We were without the leadership of a school president again and unless the board of directors could find someone soon, the school would have to be shut down. There had been at least two presidents, so far, during my four years at the school. The change in personnel was constant. Who would want to work at such a place? I remember how surprised I was that there was a board of directors. The fearful troll under the bridge once again reared his ugly head to taunt me with the prospect of no place to go. Even a bad place could at least be a place to belong.

French Camp Academy was an impossible situation. One of the most important truths I have learned in my Christian life is that—**the word "impossible" often ushers us into the doorway of the power and miraculous working of almighty God!**

— **The New Man** —

At the beginning of my freshman year in high school we were told that the school had hired a new president. We were, as always, curious about this new challenge, but never for a moment did we think he would be different. We looked forward to the chapel service in the high school auditorium, where we would get our first glimpse of this new man. I shall never forget the day. The students filed noisily into the old auditorium with its broken seats and old faded velveteen curtains hanging from the sides of the small stage in the back of the room. We laughed and taunted the teachers and staff as we put our feet up on the backs of the seats in front of us and threw spit wads at others across the room.

Then a member of the staff walked onto the stage from a side door followed by a tall red-haired man with a thousand freckles. My attention was instantly drawn to his bright flickering eyes that seemed to smile as if harboring some intimate treasured secret. As I remember that day, I realize that in the years that followed, I never saw him without that look in his eyes. I believe that those eyes that morning saw beyond our behavior and rag tag appearance to the possibility of young lives molded into the image of Jesus Christ.

We listened as he was introduced as Sam C. Patterson, the new president of French Camp Academy. As he spoke to us for the first time, his demeanor was strong, but underneath there seemed to be a gentleness that I had never seen before. There was the usual attempt at disorder from the students, but our curiosity outweighed our resolve to cause chaos. He spoke of a new school endowment as he opened his Bible to a verse from the book of Philippians and began to read: ***"And my God shall supply all your need according to His riches in glory by Christ Jesus"*** (Phil. 4:19).

At this point, we were more interested in the man than the Bible verse. How would this new challenge to our control and disruption of the school play out? Would he be strong, or would he be like all of the others—loud and threatening, but mostly all talk?

He acknowledged that the school had impossible needs, but he calmly stated that if we asked believing, God would supply every need. It was clear to everyone present that he completely believed all that he was saying. Well, that settled that! He must be as crazy as all of the others had been!

As I left the auditorium that morning, deep in my heart I detected a tiny glimmer of hope of something unexplainable, yet possible, from this unusual man with the smiling eyes.

∽2∼

"The Golden Gate Bridge"

– The Bridge of a New Life –

— Allegory —

The silhouette of a massive new bridge rises in the distance. This grand structure appears outlined against a bank of clouds that fills the landscape with shades of dark and light. This magnificent bridge's appearance is beautiful and compelling, yet rugged and strong. It's very presence seems to beckon to the heart with an unusual urgency.

As you draw near, your attention is drawn to the thick darkness beneath the bridge. The bottomless chasm below the great structure is filled with an emptiness so deep and frightening that the eye cannot even bear to search within its space for a flicker of light.

As you approach this great bridge, your heart is drawn by an unspoken, yet powerful strength to take **the next step**.

A large gate battered and challenged by the onslaught of the ages stands in the center of the bridge guarding the way across. Great hinges at its base pivot on a flaming sword of judgment, denying passage to anyone refusing to wash first in the eternal pool at its base. Scars etched deep into the gate's ancient design reveal unspeakable pain endured in its construction. Only when it swings open does the gate reveal the magnificent beauty of its golden core.

The large pillars of the bridge's foundation rest on a single rock. From this rock, massive support beams reach to heaven where they are surrounded by a great cloud that seems to watch and call to us from there to cross quickly.

"The Golden Gate Bridge"

—The Bridge of a New Life—

Many new and different things began to happen to the school after Mr. Patterson's arrival. When he walked onto the stage of the old auditorium the next morning for our scheduled chapel service, he came prepared with a list of urgent needs for the school.

The list would be endless, but the very first thing that he shared with us was that the administration building, which housed the school offices as well as the high school classrooms, did not have fire insurance. The electrical wiring was old and dangerous and needed to be replaced with new wiring. We were not at all surprised. Everything about the building was a shambles and in desperate need of repair. He shared with us the exact dollar and penny amount of the rewiring estimate (slightly over $100). He then leaned over the podium and looked at us with those smiling eyes with their strange hidden secrets as though we were deeply involved in this whole charade with him. The auditorium grew quiet as we were somehow drawn to this unusual man with the red hair. He quoted again the school's new financial endowment, *"And my God shall supply all your need according to His riches in glory by Christ Jesus,"* (Phil. 4:19).

He then amazed us by bowing his head and asking God to send us the exact amount of the rewiring cost! After his prayer, he told us that God had promised to supply this need in His Word, and that we could expect Him to answer. There was a muffled snicker that swept through the room, followed by stern looks from the coaches and staff. Well that would be the end of that—just more empty talk! I remember thinking that he had gone too far. I had secretly hoped that this new man would succeed because he appeared different from all of the others. There was a quiet, yet strong peace about him that seemed to inspire a new sense of hope in my heart.

There were chapel services in the auditorium every school day from that day on. Within a few days he walked into chapel one morning with a check in his hand for the exact amount of the rewiring cost! His eyes twinkled with the knowledge that he somehow knew that this would happen. He held up the check to us as though he expected an inspection of its contents. The check had been sent as a donation by a Sunday school class from a church in another town in Mississippi.

Now he had our attention. This began the stream of miraculous lessons in faith for our awe-struck hearts. Even the most incorrigible in our midst watched with astonishment. We were hesitant to draw any hasty conclusions about this new chain of events. After all, we each had an image of skepticism to uphold with our peers. Each new day, Mr. Patterson would present a new and specific need. Then, as always, he would pray for a specific answer from God—always quoting **Philippians 4:19** back to Him in prayer, as if reminding Him of His promise. Was this God of his toying with us?

One day, he announced to the students that the school needed a fire truck. The nearest fire station was about 30 miles away over curvy gravel roads. Once again, he bowed his head and quietly asked God to send us a fire truck. After thanking Him for supplying our every need, according to His Word, he once again dismissed us with that strange look of assurance that baffled everyone there. Now, to my amazement, I found myself secretly rooting for his God to respond quickly with an answer.

Not long after that, the fire truck appeared on campus, parked conspicuously in front of the administration building. Even though it was obviously used, its shiny red paint shone like a neon sign on our drab campus. This new evidence of God's miraculous involvement with this man electrified the whole campus. We observed this new miracle with wonder, thinking that perhaps the school had bought it somewhere. Instead, another town in Mississippi had bought a brand new truck and wanted the tax deduction that would be gained by discarding their old one with us. We were beginning to believe there was something interesting about this new man and "his prayer answering God"!

Mr. Patterson initiated a new rule for each of the students, regardless of grade or age. From now on, every student was required to take Bible as part of the curriculum. The rule was that unless you pass Bible, you do not get any other grades!

But the fact remained that, even though we studied Bible in the classroom, we were still the same misfits with broken and shattered lives as we were when Mr. Patterson arrived. We still had the same deep hurts that had spawned attitudes of rebellion and the same doubts and anger toward those in authority. I don't think any of us even knew why we were so angry inside. Perhaps it was just simply a vehicle to provide desperately needed attention. Or perhaps it was the only cry for help that our empty hearts knew how to utter.

Sometimes a hurting child will settle for even negative attention if he or she cannot get it any other way. This was the only world we had on which to vent our intense frustration and anger. I would later learn of Mr. Patterson's unfailing prayers on behalf of the hearts and lives of each of us on campus. It wasn't until after I graduated that I learned that he had prayed all of his life for an opportunity to make a difference in the lives of broken and hurting young people.

He had been a pastor for many years, but this was his heart's longing. He knew beyond any doubt that God had chosen him for this place and ministry. He also knew, beyond any doubt, that God had chosen each individual student to be at French Camp Academy. In all of the years that followed, he always insisted that each student on campus had been specifically chosen by God to be there. He moved about the campus quietly, always stopping to talk with any student that would speak to him—always finding time to listen intently to any problem or concern, no matter how trivial it seemed. And, as always, there was that disarming smile that both puzzled and drew those around him to seek out his presence. He was never afraid to approach a group of students on campus, always with an attitude of interest in each one there. Most of the teachers and staff had seemed to avoid such gatherings in the past. But, when he talked to you, he looked intently into your eyes, as though waiting for you to talk to him about something he had waited all of his life to hear. How could he possibly care? Who could understand this strange man?

Mr. Patterson announced to us in the fall of his first year at the school, that an evangelist was coming to spend a week in January, preaching and teaching in the auditorium. His name was Jimmy Johnson and he brought with him a song leader by the name of Clyde Taylor.

We were lost and broken kids that night in the old auditorium. There was nothing in us or about us that would cause anyone to want to care. In fact, most people preferred to avoid us. We did know how to make the faculty and staff miserable and we found every opportunity to make it happen. We were hurt, rejected and angry. . .and they were the only ones available that we could hurt back. We had nothing to lose.

— <u>**White as Snow**</u> —

We filed into the old auditorium to hear the first in a full week of messages by this evangelist dressed in a dark suit. The long rows of broken seats created a great deal of disruptive clatter as we banged the wooden seats noisily against their backs. This was an acceptable noisemaker for us as we snickered and stumbled over others vying for a seat next to a friend. He began talking to us about God's purpose in creation and His involvement with man down through the ages. His authority was compelling and his eyes seemed to burn right into my very soul. I knew that he could not actually see me in this sea of fidgety teens packed into the auditorium that night, but why did I feel that he was talking only to me? He talked about heaven and hell and my heart was pierced with his words. He used a large portable blackboard to chart times and future events from the Bible concerning God's judgment on the earth. He held his large black Bible high in the air to dramatize the truth of his words. We watched and listened in silence as we heard scripture read that made it clear that Jesus Christ was God's only solution for our sin, and unless the blood of Jesus Christ saved us, we would surely suffer the terrible judgment described in these passages of Scripture! I followed the sequence of scripture that unfolded before me and became deeply troubled at the sure prospects of anyone left to face such terrible judgment. As he continued he shared the amazing truth of God's wonderful gift of life, offered through the death and resurrection of His Son, Jesus Christ. As I think of these next moments, I can still feel the incredible awareness that God was calling to me personally to respond. It seemed as though I was the only person in the whole room.

The evangelist quoted from the King James Version of the Bible: ***"Come now, and let us reason together, saith the LORD: though your sins be as scarlet, they shall be as white as snow; though they be red like crimson, they shall be as wool,"*** (Isaiah 1:18).

I wanted to be as white as snow. I knew that my life was empty, and I wanted this new life that would make me new and clean. My heart seemed to scream, *"Yes!"* inside my chest! When he gave the invitation for anyone who was willing to be "born again" to come to the front of the room, I flew out of my seat and found myself standing at the base of the old stage, sobbing uncontrollably. I could not under-stand or stop the profusion of tears that seemed to wash through my whole being. Many young people came forward that night seeking this new life in Jesus Christ. I did not fully understand all of Mr. Johnson's words, but I remember Mr. Patterson asking all of us to remain there after the meeting. Then he carefully explained to us the decision we were choosing to make. All of the scriptures concerning our inheritance of sin, and the need for repentance, were carefully read and explained. Then he explained how Jesus Christ, God in the flesh, had personally taken our sin in His own body on the cross so that we might be saved from God's judgment for our sin. He asked each of us if we wanted to pray and receive Jesus Christ as our Savior and Lord. I vividly remember praying that prayer that night, along with many, many of my schoolmates. Then, before dismissing us to return to our dorms, Mr. Patterson said that we were new babies in Christ Jesus, and we needed to know how to grow and mature in understanding of our new lives. He invited all of us to meet with him in his office before breakfast the next morning to begin learning how to live and walk as new Christians.

It still takes my breath away when I think of the way God personally touched my heart. I think that perhaps, I was probably the most insignificant human being on the face of the earth and I attended the most insignificant broken-down little school, surrounded by problem kids, like myself, that no one wanted. Why would God care about us. . .or me? I have heard people comment about how God could use a particular person with special talents if that person became a Christian. This often amuses me because God is never limited or fascinated by a person's personal resume. Indeed! The great and matchless God, in His tender love looks into a person's heart. . .from the greatest this world has to offer, to the most desolate and lowliest of all, and sees a heart and life that was designed to know and walk with Him in life! He saw us with our failures and wrong choices *"before the foundation of the world"* (Eph. 1:4), and yet He still came to die in our place so that we could have eternal life with Him!

When I awoke that first morning of my new life in Christ, I was surprised to look across at my roommate sleeping in her bed across the room, as though seeing her for the first time. She had also made that wonderful journey of life toward the front of the auditorium, but why had I never really noticed her like this before? As the weeks went on, I began to realize a new dimension in my relationships with others. All of the pain and hurt in my life, up to this point, had caused me to focus entirely on me. Every circumstance, every person in my life, before that night, related only to me! I looked over at my roommate that morning, and for the first time in my life, I seemed to care about someone else besides me. I know now that unusual emotional pain in a person's life, especially at a young age, sometimes causes us to become extremely self-centered individuals. Even though I hated that selfishness in my life, I had been powerless to correct it. I could pretend to care about others, but it was always just an empty sham. There would be a long road ahead in this discovery of Christ in my life, but I was amazed at this small but new beginning. I remember wondering if my roommate was experiencing these same feelings in her life, too. Oh, I was by no means, suddenly a wonderfully congenial and likable person. I would discover that there were many bridges of healing and forgiveness that I must cross in this long journey before me. I would also learn that I would not have to make this journey alone—in fact; **I would never be alone, ever again, in my whole life**!

Many, many mornings I would quietly climb out of my bed in the darkness before dawn to dress and hurry across the short span of campus separating the two buildings, eager to learn exciting truths about my new life. My whole reason for life was beginning to change. I was given a small red testament in which I inscribed my name and the date of my new birth in Jesus Christ. There were many of us at first, but our numbers dwindled in the weeks to follow. Those early meetings on dark and cold rainy mornings were sometimes too much for me, too! The first morning that we met in Mr. Patterson's office, he talked to us about the necessity of beginning each day reading God's word and talking to Him in prayer. He began the journey of teaching us how to be men and women of faith—the same faith that he had exhibited to us by his life! He taught us to always expect God to answer abundantly every sincere, believing prayer! He said that if we only believed God for a teaspoonful, then He would answer with a teaspoonful—but if we believed God for a bucketful, then He would answer with a bucketful. My heart was thirsty for this pure and living water and I could not get my fill. We were eager to drink in all of the truth that this wonderful man of God taught us as He opened the Bible and explained the beauty and strength of our new life in Christ.

Those special times passed quickly, but we always ended on our knees on those old oiled boards, learning to pray with him for our families, the school and our new lives in Christ. I remember in the weeks

43

to follow, the fervent prayers I offered up before God's throne for my mother, my father and my stepmother—for their salvation. About 15 years ago, as I sat with my mother in her home in Mississippi, I curiously asked her exactly when she had invited Jesus Christ into her life. I knew that she had been a Christian for many, many years because we had talked often of her understanding and reliance on her Savior. She thought for awhile, and then responded with surety that it had been the spring of 1951! I gasped at the realization that her sudden urge to attend the church at the end of her street in Jackson, Mississippi, had been the direct result of my prayers before the throne of God! A few years later, after my mom passed away, my husband and I were visiting my dad and stepmother and asked them when they had accepted Christ. My stepmother quickly began telling the story of their life changing conversion through the evangelical work of a pastor and his church when they were living in Paducah, KY—in the spring of 1951!

I have learned over the years from walking with God and studying His Word, that the simple, believing prayers of a child are very powerful before the throne of God! I have often encouraged women in Bible studies that I have taught to solicit the prayers of their children in earnest prayer before God. In Roger Steer's book, George Müller: Delighted in God.[2] Mr. Steer shares wonderful examples of children in the orphanage founded and run by this great man of faith. My favorite is the story of three-year-old, Abigail, and her persistent pressure on George Müller to show her how to ask God for what she wanted. Mr. Müller picked her up and sat her on his knee and quoted from Mark 11:24 in the Bible.

"Therefore I say to you, whatever things you ask when you pray, believe that you receive them, and you will have them," (Mark 11:24).

In the account that follows, Abigail, with her small hands held together in a prayerful pose by Mr. Müller, repeats his words asking God for the wool yarn that she wants for knitting. The very next day after her prayer, a package of wool arrived in the mail that had been mailed by someone who knew of her approaching birthday and that she loved to knit. Coincidence? No! One of the most important things that Mr. Patterson taught us was that there are no coincidences in the

---

[2] George Muller: delighted in God!, by Roger Steer. Harold Shaw Publishers, Wheaton, IL, © 1975 by Roger Steer, Page 181.

life of a Christian! I believe that God delights to answer the prayers of a child.

I believe with all of my heart that when a child bows before God's throne and offers a request for God to do what He already wants to do, God will move heaven and earth to perform that task! God always seems to underscore His miracles by answering with precise timing. Perhaps, because we are such distracted sheep, we need God's precision timing to know that it has come from His hand! I believe that all of the prayers of His children are powerful before His throne, but none more powerful than the fervent, believing prayer of a child!

Looking back on the events and miracles that began to happen at French Camp Academy in the lives of the young people and the ever changing transformation of the school before our very eyes, I know with a certainty chiseled in eternity—that my God is able! A faith was forged in my heart that would become, and remain, immovable and unchanged through the many storms of life before me, because it had been carefully established on the rock of Jesus Christ and His wonderful Word. The apostle Paul has a clear warning in the Bible for anyone, who might dare to build on this great foundation with anything less than pure gold, silver or precious stones.

> *"For no other foundation can anyone lay than that which is laid, which is Jesus Christ. Now if anyone builds on this foundation with gold, silver, precious stones, wood, hay, straw, each one's work will become clear; for the Day will declare it, because it will be revealed by fire; and the fire will test each one's work, of what sort it is,"* (1 Cor. 3:11-13).

— **The Potter's Wheel** —

The whole atmosphere of the school began to change. God had begun a transformation of the school, the faculty and staff, but mostly us. Mr. Patterson began a new work program for the students that would occupy our after school hours. The School of the Ozarks in Missouri had been consulted for information about the success of their student work program. Soon Mr. Patterson began to initiate a similar plan for French Camp Academy. We did not share his enthusiasm over the new prospects of "after-school work," but it was soon obvious that we did not have a choice. He announced that every student would be assigned an area of responsibility where they would work for their room and board. Different staff members would have the responsibility to oversee students in certain areas.

All sorts of projects were soon underway. Boy's teams under the supervision of adult staff members began to be responsible for all sorts of farm jobs. As farm equipment began to be donated from farms all over the south, the boys became reluctant farm hands; learning the fine art of milking cows and how to care for pigs and horses, along with new skills like how to plow and plant corn and vegetables. They even learned how to mix and pour concrete for sidewalks. This was a massive job, indeed, for the campus seemed to float in mud. Girls under the supervision of the Home Economics teacher were soon learning to sew and new curtains began to appear in some of the windows. The girls worked in the kitchen and dining hall, and other various cleaning jobs in the dorms and administration building. Soon the wonderful smell of fresh baked bread began to permeate the upstairs floors of the girls dorm as the girls learned to do all of the school's baking. The boys would deliver fresh milk from the cows daily, and the girls, under the close supervision of the dietitian, would churn fresh butter for the dining hall. There were two wonderful cooks that had been with the school for as long as I could remember who supervised the preparation of food in the kitchen.

God continued to pour into Mr. Patterson's heart the details of His plan for this "impossible" school that God had chosen for a trophy of His love. Many amazing miracles happened in the years to come, but we were no longer surprised. We had now been convinced that this was God's school, and we were "God's kids" chosen for His use.

I was fortunate enough to work in Mr. Patterson's office after school, mainly because I passed typing. The biggest part of my job was typing thank you letters for the many, many contributions that began to pour into the school. Mr. Pat, as he was often called, would have a letter of special thanks written out in longhand that he wanted me to type for each person, or group, in the stacks of gifts received. These letters always included stories of ways that God was moving in the lives of these students with broken lives and hearts. Each month the letter was different, but always giving praise to God for His amazing faithfulness to perform according to the promises in His Word. After signing each letter personally he would then write a special note on each one expressing his personal appreciation. It seemed to me that he must know everyone in the whole world. My typing on the old typewriter was embarrassing and the letters were often filled with black smudges from erasing the mistakes between the crinkled sheets of much used carbons. If he came into the office when I was there, I often apologized for the many obvious mistakes, but he only smiled and thanked me for my good work!

So much of his new vision depended on sharing God's purpose for the school with other churches. He traveled tirelessly, telling anyone who would listen, of the school's vision to provide a Christian home for special young people with broken lives. If he was out of town speaking to other churches or groups, the piles of thank you letters grew on his desk. I had the privilege of seeing firsthand how God responds to one man's walk of faith! What an impact this made on my life!

Something very unusual began to happen with the students. Yes, there was much grumbling at first. There were always some that balked at the hard work, but as we were given the responsibility to work and complete difficult jobs on which the school depended, we began to develop a sense of accomplishment in all that we were doing. Yes, we even began to feel that we had somehow become important to the school! I had never felt important, or needed, by anyone before in my whole life. The seeds of self-worth were beginning to sprout in some of our lives!

— **Psalm 27:10** —

The next school year, 1951-52, Mr. Johnson, the evangelist, returned to the school for another series of meetings. While he was there, one particular day I happened to be sitting on the bench that circled the trunk of an old cottonwood tree in front of the girl's dormitory. This was a sort of designated place where, as girls, we waited for just the right boy to happen by. Instead, the evangelist in the black suit approached and sat down beside me. Of course, that ended any chance of talking with the handsome young man as he hurried past on his way to the dining hall. I was a sophomore in high school at the time and Mr. Johnson pointedly asked me if I had made plans for college? I was so caught off guard that I responded with shock and laughter. I quickly told him that there was no way that I could even think of college. There was no one in the whole world that could afford such a thing, and especially for me!

Mr. Johnson calmly said, "If God wants you in college, He will send you!"

— The Unbelievable Miracle —

1 Corinthians 2:9 says, *"Eye has not seen, nor ear heard, Nor have entered into the heart of man The things which God has prepared for those who love Him."* The wonderful thing is that even before we know God's Word as it applies to us, it is still true!

The following week, Mr. Johnson was scheduled to hold a series of meetings in Meridian, Mississippi and had requested that our student Glee Club come to sing at the end of his last service. I happened to be in the Glee Club, and was happy that I would be able to hear Mr. Johnson one more time. I admired him a great deal and loved hearing his forceful preaching that demanded attention to God's wonderful plan of salvation.

After the service was over that evening, some of us walked across the room to say goodbye to him because we knew he would not be back for another year. Just as I reached his elbow, a well-dressed man stepped up to him and said, *"Mr. Johnson, I would like to send some young person to college through you!"*

Mr. Johnson's response as he wheeled around and took me by the arm was, *"Sir, here is the girl!"* I was introduced to the elderly couple who assured me that they would be in touch with Mr. Patterson to make the necessary arrangements after I made a decision about my choice for a school. I was overwhelmed. My heart and mind were whirling with this sudden, thrilling possibility of God's blessing and favor toward me. Why me? I was nobody—less than nobody in my eyes. As I wondered about this new and wonderful turn in my life, God showed me a passage in His Word one morning during my daily devotions,

> *"But God has chosen the foolish things of the world to put to shame the wise, and God has chosen the weak things of the world to put to shame the things which are mighty; and the base things of the world and the things which are despised God has chosen, and*

*the things which are not, to bring to nothing the things
that are, that no flesh should glory in His presence"*
(1 Cor.1:27-29).

I marked these verses with a red pencil. During times of discouragement I would often open my Bible to this passage and lay it on the bed in front of me and remember this amazing expression of my Savior's love and responsibility to me—and for me as His own! I was struck with the realization that God had sought to make it clear to me that the prayer I had cried out to Him as a little lost girl of 10, had been heard and answered. He had provided **a home and a family** for me for all eternity! My home now was with Him, and He would be my family! James Ryle, a former pastor of a church that I attended in Boulder, Colorado, wrote in his book, "Hippo in the Garden,"[3] how God cared for him in every way, as an earthly father would. A few years later, while thanking God for being his Father, he questioned God as to the identity of his spiritual mother. God spoke to him clearly that the church had acted as his mother—always nurturing, teaching and supporting him as he matured in Christ. This is a wonderful picture of God's promise in Psalm 27:10, *"When my father and my mother forsake me, Then the LORD will take care of me."*

God's faithfulness toward me has been more than any earthly father's could ever be. He has never failed to correct me when I am bent on going my own stubborn way, nor has He ever failed to love me and supply my every need!

Later that year, Mr. Patterson's wife, Estelle, offered to help me in the selection of a Christian college. Her offer of assistance was a lifesaver. The only Christian colleges that I had heard of were very large and, somewhat threatening, for this little girl from nowhere. She told me about the wonderful Christian women's college that she had attended in the Blue Ridge Mountains of North Carolina and said that she would be glad to write to them for brochures and catalogs. She sent away to other schools, as well, but I was completely captivated by the pictures of the beautiful campus covered with pink and white dogwood, nestled within such beautiful mountains. None of the other catalogs even remotely interested me after I saw that one. I also liked

---

[3] Hippo in the Garden, Creation House, Orlando, FL. © 1993 by James Ryle. Page 86-87.

the idea of attending a woman's college (with several Christian men's colleges close by).

We settled on Montreat College, 16 miles west of Asheville, NC, in the Blue Ridge Mountains of Western North Carolina. Every time I thought about this impossible dream becoming a reality for me, my heart pounded with fear. I could barely remember a life beyond these walls—how could I possibly think of attending college with *normal kids*. Was this really going to happen to me? Would I fail these wonderful people who seemed to believe in me? Mr. Patterson reminded me that God's Word says, *"I can do all things through Christ who strengthens me"* (Phil. 4:13).

My senior year in high school, the wonderful couple in Meridian, MS, came and picked me up for the weekend. They took me with them to Meridian where we spent several days shopping and trying on clothes for college. As I returned to French Camp Academy, I felt like Cinderella, only instead of being touched by a fairy godmother's wand, the loving hand of my Father in heaven had touched me once again with His provision. My benefactor's had even purchased a full set of beautiful luggage for my new college adventure!

French Camp Academy today, with its teeming student body and beautiful campus, stands as a trophy of praise to God's faithfulness to His Word. It still has as its only financial endowment, Philippians 4:19. The large dormitories have been replaced by many smaller homes built to house 12 to 14 students. The house parents are Christian couples chosen by God to love and care for the young people in each one.

The school still only accepts young people from broken and disadvantaged backgrounds and each one is still required to work for their room and board. But the campus today is filled with students that God has chosen to touch in a special way with His great love.

In 1974, I had made plans to visit my mother in Crystal Springs, MS, and decided to also attend my 20th reunion at the school. Mr. Patterson had been called by God to start a new Seminary in Jackson, MS and the new school president, Stuart Angle, offered me the opportunity to share my testimony with the students, as well as teaching time in the classroom. The school had completed new apartments for visitors in some of the old rooms of Alexander Strange Memorial that had once been the boy's dorm on "the hill." The room that I stayed in was beautifully furnished and very comfortable, but it brought to mind many stories that I had heard about this infamous place in "the old days."

The students had been informed that anyone, who wished to spend counseling time with me for those evenings, would be issued special passes to leave their dorms. One evening, as I sat in my room reading, there was a hesitant tap at my door. As I opened the door, I saw a tall blond young man who seemed to be about 16 or 17. He seemed shy and a little embarrassed that he was there. I invited him into the room and offered him a seat on the chair next to the couch where I had been sitting. He offered me the slip of paper granting him permission to be there and asked if he could talk to me. I smiled at him, thinking that he must be an athlete and quickly breathed up a silent prayer for God to help me see beyond the façade that I knew I would encounter. His face flushed as he began, revealing his difficulty with the planned questions. I stopped him and told him that whatever he planned to say was not the real reason he was there. He confessed that a group of boys had dared him to come with the purpose of pretending to need answers to outrageous questions that were designed to embarrass me. It was supposed to be a terrific joke for the boys waiting back at his dorm! I smiled at him, reminding him that I, too, had once been in his shoes. Even as he had entered the door, my heart seemed to know him and his need to mask his true feelings. I knew that God had brought him, for I had prayed that God would bring only those students prepared by God. We bowed our heads and asked God to direct our conversation. Within moments, we were on our knees together, as Wylie tearfully prayed for Jesus Christ to come into his heart. A few years later someone told me that at Wylie's high school graduation, he shared with the school the life-changing encounter that had backfired that night and led him to Christ. What a privilege to have been a part of that young man's appointment with God.

Over the years, Wylie and hundreds of other young people that the world has labeled as "hopeless" have encountered the life changing experience of turning their lives over to Jesus Christ through the tender and loving hands of God's chosen ambassadors at this wonderful school. Many, many of them now serve Jesus Christ in full-time Christian service as pastors', educators and leaders in many professions.

How I thank God that He led me to this little school with its muddy barren campus so many years ago.

> *"For I know the thoughts that I think toward you,*
> *says the LORD, thoughts of peace and not of evil, to*
> *give you a future and a hope. Then you will call upon*
> *Me and go and pray to Me, and I will listen to you. And*
> *you will seek Me and find Me, when you search for Me*
> *with all your heart"* (Jer. 29:11-13).

This magnificent bridge with its Golden Gate has been designed and built by the Master Builder, Himself, and must be crossed by each of us if we would journey with Him to His home in heaven. The battered and scarred gate beckons to our hearts to make the life changing choice to open its great door, leading to eternal life. Jesus says in the book of The Revelation,

> *"Behold, I stand at the door and knock. If anyone*
> *hears My voice and opens the door, I will come in to*
> *him and dine with him, and he with Me,"* (Rev. 3:20).

There is no other way to cross the great chasm of judgment for our sin, required by God's holiness, except through God's Son, Jesus Christ. The hand of God beckoned to me that night in that old dingy auditorium, offering to me a lifetime of peace and hope in this world, as well as life with Him for all eternity! The miracle of His life-changing love is offered to each one of us, no matter who we are or how we grew up. I have looked deep into the hearts of broken and troubled young people across the country and said, "If you were the only person on this earth, Jesus Christ would still have died on that cross for you!" I know that it is true, because He reached out His hand and healed my broken and shattered life that the world had labeled as "unwanted."

A few years ago, while visiting some of my family in Mississippi, I grew very sad as I listened to childhood memories that were being shared between my dad, my stepmother, and my brother; memories that I had not had the privilege of sharing. I quietly left the room, troubled at how quickly and deeply this old hurt still surfaced in my heart. God then began to remind me that He had chosen me for His own special possession and that it had been His perfect plan to send me to this little broken down school where I would find the priceless gift of salvation through the tender love of Jesus Christ. It had also been my great privilege to learn of God's kingdom at the feet of one of the greatest men that I have ever known. My focus was instantly corrected with a heart of overwhelming gratitude for God's perfect plan in my life. Jesus says in the gospel of John, *"I am the way, the truth, and the life. No one comes to the Father except through Me,"* (John 14:6).

No one else can open the gate for you, but as you choose to place your hand on the golden handle, the beautiful gate swings open, as though, waiting all of your life for you to enter.

There are many bridges in each of our lives, but none so beautiful in design — so exciting in promise — so complete in accomplishment, — and so necessary for life, as this one with the golden gate.

໑3ໝ

"London Bridge, Falling Down"
— The Bridge of Self Exaltation —

— Allegory —

The roar of a mighty river can be heard in the distance suggesting another bridge to be crossed. Warning signs of structural weakness appear at intervals along the side of the path, but are easily brushed aside as this new and imposing bridge comes into full view. This new bridge seems to beckon with promises of success and favor, causing you to quicken your step in its direction.

Confusing signposts point to another bridge, but the path in that direction is narrow and the bridge is barely noticeable in the distance. The choice seems easy as your gaze is drawn to the promising path before you.

This new bridge rises in majestic splendor as a large imposing structure spanning the distance across the great river before you. There are no apparent hindrances at the entrance to this bridge, and the way is broad and smooth, making it strikingly different from the others. The spans are extravagant and reasonable in their design and seem to rise before you as though constructed out of your own imagination.

Many attractive diversions and amusements now dot the landscape promising rewards and recognition for those who travel this bridge.

The foundation is surprisingly shallow for such a massive bridge and the riverbed below the crossing seems at first glance to be only sand. However, the promise of success for an easy crossing is attractive and the way seems easy.

Weathered signposts on either side of the entrance warn of the threat of quicksand and the possibility of collapse for any structure built at this site, but all warnings are brushed aside in eager determination to experience this new adventure.

Subtle changes in the bridges structure are barely noticeable until you begin to stumble on the ruts and cracks that begin to appear in the once smooth surface. This beautiful bridge that was so full of promise and easy solutions has now become shadowed in struggle and conflict. You begin to spend more and more time wishing you had paid closer attention to the warning signs that appeared on the path.

The bridge shudders and quakes with the weight of the wind and storms that have now begun to threaten its foundation. The once peaceful and fulfilling journey has become one of exhausting struggle against the cold winds of confusion. The exit from this bridge appears empty and frightening in the distance. Disappointment and regret burden the one who began with such confidence and resolve. Why had I ignored the warnings about this bridge? Would I ever find my way back across this river?

"London Bridge, Falling Down"

—The Bridge of Self Exaltation—

When the old Greyhound bus that was to take me to this new adventure pulled into the station in Asheville, North Carolina, my heart was pounding in my chest so loud that the noise seemed stifling.

God had provided the miracle of college for me through a Christian couple in Meridian, Mississippi, and this was to begin a new adventure in my life! How did this scared little girl from nowhere ever get so far from the muddy, rain soaked little campus in Mississippi? I was sure that this was all a dream and someone would call my name and tell me that they had meant to send someone else to this beautiful place.

The little school of French Camp Academy now seemed light years away, but the wonderful miracle by God to provide a college education for me would always be indelibly stamped in my heart.

Montreat College for Women was a "dream come true" for me. It had been chosen with the help of Mr. Patterson's wife, Estelle, who had also attended this beautiful school. I would learn many new lessons during this new part of my life; some of them academic, but many of them would be about myself and my stubborn resolve to *"do it my way!"*

Every moment of every day from then on was an exhilarating new experience. A pleasant man in a station wagon met me at the bus station and piled the old metal trunk and my beautiful new matching luggage into the back end of the car. The car left the station and turned out on the highway toward my new life. The majestic mountains were spread out on either side of the highway like far away wisps of smoke in the distance. The driver finally turned off at a sign announcing the road to Black Mountain, North Carolina. Nothing in my whole life had ever prepared me for the beauty of the drive before me. Montreat College was, and is, nestled in the beautiful Blue Ridge Mountains of western North Carolina. When the staff member left the main highway at Black Mountain and began the short drive to Montreat College, the mountains that had seemed so smoky from a distance now took on a profusion of colors that took my breath away. The pink and white dogwood trees dressed in their most brilliant autumn reds and oranges bowed as we passed, while the flaming reds of the maples and tulip trees seemed to shout in their own chorus of praise to the Creator for a job "well done!" The fall colors of the rhododendron and mountain laurel that grew wild in the underbrush were everywhere like wildfire that swept across the landscape unhindered. How could I contain my composure in the presence of such beauty? If heaven is more beautiful than this (and I know it will be), it will take us the first thousand years to catch our breath!

As the old station wagon wound along the narrow curvy road between the mountains and valleys, the softness of the trees and underbrush seemed to rise on either side like a brilliant palette waiting for the Master's brush. Finally, the deep underbrush seemed to sweep us into a meadow in preparation for heaven's parlor that was just beyond. A narrow stone gate was arched across the road ahead as if announcing to the world that "not just anyone" could proceed beyond this point. The driver drew me back to the reality of the moment by stating that we had arrived at our destination. My heart began to pound again and I thought that I might be sick. The road was now peppered with driveways leading to small quaint houses built with the same beautiful stone as the arched gate. Side roads disappeared into the underbrush at intervals as if leading to some secret hideaway beyond reality. Just as I was convinced that I had seen all of the beautiful landscape allotted to me for a lifetime, the station wagon rounded a curve and my mouth dropped. I had arrived at Shangri-La. Nestled in a panorama of beauty stood massive buildings that looked like castles in some imaginary fairy tale. These stone castles were tucked into the hillsides surrounding a crystal clear lake at its center. Water cascading over the lake's spillway seemed to dance with a thousand diamonds as it fell to the moss covered stones below. The gurgling mountain stream that had led us along the road from the stone entrance sang a welcome to my heart as the car wound through the campus to a stone building on the far side of the lake. The car pulled into the great stone portico where the driver began unloading my belongings. As I stepped from the car and saw the beautiful place that was to be my new home, my heart almost stopped. I had stepped from one lifetime into another universe!

The interior walls of the lobby were made of stones that looked as if they were filled with thousands of shimmering crystals. Great pillars that sparkled and glittered with this same stone supported the ceiling of the massive room. Between the huge windows looking down to the valley below, was a fireplace large enough to hold a small car. The interior of the firebox was black with soot from roaring fires that had easily warmed the beautiful lobby.

Our meals were served in a stone building on the far side of the lake. Assembly Inn was the convention center for the church conferences in the summer and was large and very elegant. As we climbed the massive stone steps leading to the dining room on the second floor, the beauty of this new world struck me again. The stairway we had just climbed could easily have been the one where Cinderella lost her glass slipper leaving the ball. Would I, too, wake up now and find that this was all a dream? In the years to follow, we would attend many beautiful teas and receptions in this elegant place. The large dining room with its immaculate white tablecloths and glittering stone pillars looked down on the whole valley below through large arched windows. From there I could see the full panorama of the campus with its large stone buildings reflected in the shimmering lake and the profusion of dogwood trees that graced the beautifully manicured lawns. In the summer, these beautiful grounds bustled with church meetings and activities for delegates and their families from all over the south.

I felt like I had reached the end of the rainbow and the "pot of gold" was the promise of happiness ever after! How could disappointment and heartache ever touch me again? God had proven His love for me and my Christian life would now be the answer to all of my life's deepest longings. I had witnessed miracles at the hands of my prayer answering Father in heaven. What more could I ever need?

Little did I know that I had just entered the doorway to one of the toughest learning experiences of my Christian life? God does not want us to remain baby Christians that always have to be fed on milk (1 Cor. 3:1-3); protected from every little pebble in our path. He wants us to learn to face life with the strength and wisdom to make the choices that will grow us into mature, strong Christians. I thought this wonderful new college experience was to be a bed of spiritual roses, but God's plan was more like "Welcome to, 'Time to grow up, 101!'"

When my children were little babies I protected them and cared for their every need. Never would I approach one of my little ones in the crib and demand that they get up and come to the table for a steak dinner. I made sure that no demands were made on their young lives that would be too much for them to handle. As they began to grow as toddlers, I carefully watched out for the possibility of danger at every turn, keeping a careful watch over their world so that they could develop into healthy strong young women. The day then came when I could teach them to walk and talk and progress to the next level of training in their lives. This is the way God trains you and me to grow up in our Christian life. He never takes us too far too fast. But, He will not allow us to remain comfortable in the nest when we should be learning to soar in the heavens!

I am reminded of the mother eagle that builds her nest high in the rocks or tops of trees so that dangerous predators cannot reach the young birds. While the nest is under construction, however, she binds it together with sharp thorns and other objects that she then covers with soft feathers. While the baby chicks are very young the feathers provide a soft and comfortable environment for their young bodies. However, as the baby eaglets begin to mature the mother begins to remove the soft padding so that the young birds will no longer be comfortable in the nest and will then begin to venture out on the surrounding limbs or rocks. This is a painful example of "tough love" in the life of the eaglets. The mother eagle instinctively knows that the young birds need a little encouragement to venture out from the warm soft nest where they have been fed and cared for by their parent. This is a wonderful example of the spiritual "push" that our heavenly Father sometimes has to give us to make us leave our "leaning post" and begin to walk and talk as growing, maturing Christians.

I have talked with so many new Christians that have been baffled by the seemingly sudden absence of God's doting ways that they enjoyed as brand new baby Christians. Comments like, "God used to answer all of my prayers. . .what has happened? Have I done something wrong?" The answer, of course, is that now it is time for you to learn to stand on your own spiritual legs and begin the process of learning to trust God in new and mature ways. This can be a real shock to our system, but will yield rich abundant fruit in our Christian walk in years to come.

In addition to normal growing pains, some of us have a strong independent streak of "Please, God. . .I'd rather do it myself." In other words, I had a serious attitude problem. God saw this in my heart and knew that it would take "spiritual surgery" to pry my death grip loose from the independent self-sufficiency that permeated my heart.

I was one of God's stubborn, independent children that felt that God was probably relieved to have a child that could handle things without constant watching. I was in for a real shock!

I have learned during the years of struggle and head *"butting against the goad"* (Acts 26:14), that God is very willing to take as much time as needed in our lives to make sure we learn the important lessons thoroughly. My college career turned out to be the training ground perfectly suited to show me my stubborn self-will, and how deadly it can be if left unchecked in the Christian life. Rarely does a new Christian realize the truth of the great and real transaction that has taken place in heaven when he or she made the decision to accept Jesus Christ as Savior (1 Cor. 6:20). At the moment of salvation, we were redeemed (rescued from spiritual death) by God the Father and made heirs and joint-heirs with Jesus Christ of God's kingdom for all of eternity. God has become our heavenly parent and takes His responsibility to us and for us very seriously.

My strong self-willed independence was so deeply rooted in my life that I think that all God had to do was stand back and watch while I dashed head-long into the self-destruct mode of my life. I did not realize there was anything wrong in my heart.

A brand new Christian often comes packaged with many wrong ideas about God and the way God expects one of His children to live. Mr. Patterson taught us so much about God's Word and how to trust Him, but somehow I missed the part about allowing Jesus Christ to run things and be the "Lord of my life". I thought that reading my Bible, praying, and "being good," would be all that was required. The rest was up to me. I set out to be all that this wonderful world of Christian academia admired and rewarded. I wanted those "back at the ranch," so to speak, to be proud of me. My purpose was to excel in every phase of my college career.

The apostle Paul writes to the young church in Corinth about this very problem:

> *"And I, brethren, could not speak to you as to spiritual people but as to carnal, as to babes in Christ. I fed you with milk and not with solid food; for until now you were not able to receive it, and even now you are still not able; for you are still carnal. "For where there*

are envy, strife, and divisions among you, are you not carnal and behaving like mere men?" (1 Cor. 3:1-4).

The word "carnal" here means "fleshly." This means that we are still living to please our wants and/or desires instead of seeking to live for God and what He wants our lives to be. Even though he knew that he was writing to Christians, they had not left the worlds "lordship" behind. They were either untaught about needing to make Jesus Christ Lord of their lives, or they were still trying to lead a double life. They had not yet discovered that even the best that the world could offer could not satisfy the deepest longings of a heart that was designed only for God.

Jesus says in Matthew 6:24,

"No one can serve two masters; for either he will hate the one and love the other, or else he will be loyal to the one and despise the other. You cannot serve God and mammon."

The word "mammon" in this verse comes from an Aramaic word for "riches", also a Hebrew word for "treasure". Clearly, Jesus knows our heart! We may soothe our thoughts with the notion that we dwell somewhere in the middle, but God's Word chillingly declares otherwise.

Many years ago I can remember hearing a beautiful young woman with Campus Crusade for Christ say, "we each have a 'God shaped vacuum' in our heart that can only be filled by Jesus Christ." The purpose of this descriptive picture is to show that God designed each of us to be indwelled by God, the Creator, made known through the person of Jesus Christ, who comes to live in our hearts when we receive Jesus Christ as our personal Savior. My own experiences have proven this to be absolutely true!

We try to satisfy the deep longings in our lives with other things such as a college degree; marriage; children; travel; work; hobbies, etc. With each accomplishment, we find that there is still a mysterious emptiness in our heart. No matter how hard we try—experiences, relationships, things, riches, etc., even good things, still leave us with a longing inside. We were made to be indwelled by God! (John 14:17; Col. 1:27) Nothing else will satisfy until this real and ultimate need of the human heart is complete in Jesus Christ! This is the way we were designed. We may try to convince ourselves that achievement of our special dreams will produce happiness ever after, but time will reveal that the emptiness is still there.

This is why the divorce rate is off the charts. We seek the perfect mate to fulfill happiness, but we soon find that, no matter how wonderful, or how successful, or how nice that person is, there is something missing. The answer is not in "the perfect mate". . .the answer is in our own heart's need to be filled by Jesus Christ.

I was certain that my college experience would be the ultimate satisfaction for me. I poured myself into this climb for success with excitement and enthusiasm. I was determined to be the best that this college had ever seen. Without realizing what I was doing, I think that the possibility of proving to the world that this little lost girl from nowhere could be somebody began to consume my life! I needed to prove—perhaps to myself; perhaps to peers; perhaps to the world that had rejected me—that I was a "keeper" and not a "throw-away."

I began to pour myself into leadership opportunities and relished the praise that each new accomplishment afforded me. The trust and recognition from classmates, faculty and staff became an elixir that began to soothe and stroke my stunted and battered ego with pride. I did not know or understand at the time that I had started out on a path of self-exaltation that would threaten to undermine my walk with Jesus Christ. When I invited Him to come into my heart at the age of 15, I was totally and completely bankrupt—spiritually, physically and emotionally. When God promised to my heart that night that I could be "white as snow" (Isaiah 1:18), I was compelled by God's Holy Spirit to respond. Jesus Christ miraculously came into my heart and began the life-long process of transforming my life. I thought that was all there was to it! Many new and wonderful changes began to occur. There was overwhelming evidence of His love and supernatural plan for my life and I began to feel His intervention and protection over me. But no one had warned me about the dangers ahead of trying to run my own life! After all, wouldn't God be pleased that I was taking charge of things? The independence that had developed in my life from the age of 10 had been a strong factor in my survival at French Camp Academy and was now rooted deep in my personality. The wall of protection that I had built around myself, though penetrated by my Savior, would prove as a barrier to His Lordship in my life. I saw this independence as an asset, but God saw it as deadly and dangerous in my walk with Him.

When Jesus Christ comes to live in a heart, He desires to become the center of that life. He then begins to work all things in our lives together according to His plan and direction for us. The Bible says, *"For I know the thoughts that I think toward you, says the LORD, thoughts of peace and not of evil, to give you a future and a hope"* (Jer. 29:11).

I had the mistaken idea that God would perhaps be pleased with my plans. I knew that you should pray for God to provide a miracle if you needed help. I also knew that I was supposed to ask Him to supply my needs, which He did in abundance. But no one told me that I needed to ask Him what His plans were for my life **before** I launched my own. I guess that I thought that my plans were His plans. Wasn't it enough to be a Christian? How could I get into trouble with God as long as I toed the mark? I somehow expected God to endorse my plans and make them work. This may sound a little silly or ridiculous to someone reading this, especially if you have not yet seen this in your own life. The truth is, this is the nature of *self* in each of our hearts, and while it may manifest itself in different ways, it is the same for all of us. It always seeks to "run the show", so to speak.

The Bible says, *". . .you were bought at a price;"* (1 Cor. 6:20). When Jesus Christ comes to live in a heart, He not only accepts responsibility to that person, but He also accepts responsibility for that person. It is now His plan to nurture and grow us in our new life so that we will become the person of character and strength that He desires for us to be. Our own ideas and plans are flawed and warped by selfish desires and ideals that will eventually cause us harm, and stunt our growth into Christ-likeness. I found this out the hard way.

How wonderful that God is the One who is the *"author and the finisher of our faith!"* (Heb. 12:2). He is committed to transforming our lives into the "image of Jesus Christ". (2 Cor. 3:18), and **He is not in a hurry**! His ways are often painful and hard, for He is dealing with stubborn and difficult sheep! The Bible makes this clear in Isaiah 55:8. He tells us that He does not think the way we think, and His ways of accomplishing something are not the same way that we would do it. This is a broad paraphrase of the verse, but He has time and time again seemed to spell it out in my life. When God sets out to accomplish a change in my life, He does it in such a way that I cannot possibly miss the lesson. However, if I do miss it the first time because of stubborn blindness on my part, He continues the lesson over and over until I finally do get it!

When I look back on the rough edges that God saw in my heart, I can almost imagine Him rolling up His sleeves in preparation for the challenge ahead.

At the end of my freshman year the Dean of Women, called me into her office and told me that my benefactor in Meridian, Mississippi had suffered a serious physical health problem and could not continue with tuition support for the next year. My heart almost stopped. To be denied continuation of this dream was unthinkable to me! Then she assured me that the college had decided that it would subsidies my continuing education with other scholarships. I was speechless with gratitude for the confidence these wonderful people had shown in me. As hard as I worked, I still could not believe that I deserved this kind of favor.

There is a verse in Psalm 27, verse 10 that says, *"When my father and my mother forsake me, then the Lord will take care of me."* This has been so very true in my life! Not only has He assumed the responsibility to supply my every need, but also He has provided outstanding mentors to teach and guide me through life's checks and balances. No, it has not always been rosy, for I have stubbornly made many mistakes, but His sure discipline has also been faithful.

These blessings continued throughout the remainder of my college life. However, as I continued in my college career, my time and passion for fellowship with God began to suffer. Soon, daily Bible reading and prayer began to be squeezed into a back corner of my busy schedule. I did not mean for this to happen. I did not even know when or why it happened. My days were jammed with classes, and responsibilities in each of the assistant categories, plus sports and other extra curriculum activities. Weekends were jammed with science labs that filled my Saturday mornings and afternoons. Evenings usually meant overseeing the gymnasium for roller skating, basketball practice, calling a square dance for visiting church groups, or refereeing one of the intramural games—unless there was another science lab to attend. After locking the gymnasium at 10 p.m., then I would walk back to the dormitory to begin my studies. Priorities for the things of God were replaced with the priorities of self. When this happens in the life of a Christian the old habits and appetites begin to return. Hence, the verse already quoted in 1 Corinthians 3:1. Yes, we are "born again", but we have settled for a life that Paul describes as Carnal, or worldly. However, now it is a life filled with confusion and misery because we are trying to live in two worlds (Gal. 5:17).

I am sure that others who watched my life thought that all was smooth and unruffled as I continued through this maze of responsibility. During my freshman year, I had set my goal to accomplish a particular role of leadership by the time I reached my senior year. As you can probably guess by now, it did not happen. My heart problem by now was deeper than just this particular incident in my life. We often have difficulty seeing what is going on with us until God presents a demonstration of the real heart issue. My confident exterior and togetherness had begun to show serious cracks and I felt exposed and naked before my peers. The pain and rejection that had defined my life before I met Jesus Christ ripped at my heart all over again. In an attempt to protect my shattered pride, I once again retreated inside the wall of protection called **"I really don't care-ism."** How could I have left myself this vulnerable, this open and exposed, to so much hurt? So many questions pounded my heart and I felt lost and alone.

For the first time, I began to be aware that something was seriously wrong in my own heart. We fail to recognize that God is more concerned with the finished product in our lives. This pain is for a time, but God looks down through the months and years to see the possibility of mature, strong Christians. He does not want us to remain "spoiled children" who can only be content when we get our own way. I had not realized before how driven I had been—or why. It was as if I had taken the wrong road, but had somehow lost the map. I stumbled and searched for answers, but could not yet understand the predicament of my heart. Wasn't God pleased with me? How could I have gotten so caught up in wanting something so much? I knew there was nothing wrong with the goal; the problem was that I was set on accomplishing my own plans, in my own way, in my own time. I had long ago left God completely out of my planning agenda. Now this disappointing incident dangled like a mirror before my heart, revealing just how far I had drifted away from His love and direction in my life. I felt like I had failed myself, those who had invested so much faith in me, and most of all, God!

A few years ago I heard the pastor of the church I attended say that Satan will be content to move us off center just a little because he knows that this slight compromise will result in a broad span that takes us far from God in years to come. I know that this is true. The enemy is patient because he knows that a little compromise will eventually lead to large compromises in our lives. All we need do is "take the path of least resistance." God is committed to each one of us to make sure we grow and mature in our new walk with Him, and He warns us in His Word, the Bible, to be watchful and obey His leading. We must be careful not to chart our own course, or sure danger lies ahead in our path. God desires to keep this from happening through roadblocks and discipline from the very beginning. We can stubbornly insist on going our own way, but it will cause great damage and pain in our own lives, and often in the lives of our families.

Even after all of this, I was not yet willing to admit to myself that I had taken the wrong bridge. In referring to the "wrong bridge", I do not mean my college experience. . .I mean my stubborn independence in "running my own life, my way!"

Later in the same spring, I was nominated and elected as president of the senior class for the coming year and quickly poured myself into the planning for my class and the legacy we would leave to the school. By the time my senior year arrived, I was thoroughly confused about the lack of peace that I felt in my heart. Every part of my life was beginning to suffer. Now and then I would steal away to the little prayer chapel and search my heart to find the reason for such insecurity. One day I encountered another girl in my class in that quiet place who even sought to reach out to me with her counsel. I quickly rebuffed her touch. After all, who did she think she was? My pride would not allow me to admit my need for help. I was exhausted, mentally, physically, emotionally and spiritually! This wonderful girl will never know how often I wished that my pride and independence had not stopped me from accepting her love that day. But I could not risk being vulnerable to anyone. That wall around my heart had been rebuilt, stronger than ever.

When Jesus Christ first comes into a person's heart, all of the parts of a life begin to work in harmony because for the first time, God is in control. He is determined to guide and protect His "new born". When we get past the baby stage in our growth, we begin to make choices that can affect the direction of our lives. When we ignore His careful guidance and direction, we will begin to drift away from His fellowship. Things begin to go wrong and if we persist in this direction, our lives will begin to once again take on the characteristics of our lives before we knew Jesus Christ.

No, this does not mean that we lose our salvation. When a person makes a conscious decision to receive Jesus Christ as Savior, a transaction takes place in Heaven. Jesus offers His spotless blood on God's altar as payment for that person's sin; God accepts Jesus' blood, and that person's sin is blotted out before God (Rev. 13:8). That person passes from death to life. But, God knows that we are weak and fail so many times. That is why He tells us in 1 John 1:9, *"If we confess our sins, He is faithful and just to forgive us our sins and to cleanse us from all unrighteousness."* When we are careful to confess our sin to God, the Bible says that He will forgive us and we will be able to continue in spotless fellowship with Him. Hebrews 13:5 says, *"For He Himself has said 'I will never leave you nor forsake you.'"*

If we stubbornly persist in going our own way, we then, become what the Bible calls in 1 Corinthians 3:3 as carnal or worldly Christians. This is a dangerous place for the Christian, for we leave ourselves vulnerable to the enemy. 1 Peter 5:7-8 says, *"Be sober, be vigilant, because your adversary the devil walks about like a roaring lion, seeking whom he may devour."* When Satan finds a Christian who is out from under the protection of God's wings (Ps. 91:4) because of un-confessed sin in his life, he is sure to cause unhindered havoc in that life. That is why God warns us over and over in His Word to be watchful—to be careful to *"keep our hearts with all diligence"* (Prov. 4:23-27).

As graduation approached, I was eager to move on with my future, but was deeply saddened to see this part of my life end. The last semester of my senior year was filled with practice teaching in science and physical education in a small mining town about 30 miles from the college. The students that I taught were mostly under-privileged teens of coal miners living in the rugged mountains surrounding the town. Some of the boys were older than I was and eager to test my ability to keep discipline. This new experience was rich, indeed, but when I finished, I felt that any other teaching job would be "a piece of cake" by comparison!

In May of that year, I was awarded a BS degree in Science and Physical Education by the faculty and staff of the college. Before the year was out I accepted an offer for the beginning of the next year to teach science in a junior high school in Jackson, Mississippi.

Women, at times, have asked me why God did not stop them from making mistakes that seriously affected certain parts of their lives. Yes, God could have stopped me from taking the wrong bridge across this river. And, yes!, the consequences of my stubborn, willful decisions were costly and painful, but I wonder if I would have ever realized how much I needed God's strength alone, instead of my own, if I had not been allowed to continue. Our loving God knows just how far each of us must go to learn the painful lessons that always result when we, "do it our way!" After pleading with God three times to remove an infirmity that plagued his life, Paul tells us in his letter to the Corinthians, that God's answer to him was, *"My grace is sufficient for you, for My strength is made perfect in weakness"* (2 Cor. 12:9).

There have been times in my life when I have felt His doors slam shut to keep me from making wrong decisions. But it was not until I became a parent myself that I fully understood why God sometimes allows us to make wrong decisions that later cause us deep pain and heartache. I learned that a loving parent must, at times, allow his or her child to fail in order to teach them vital lessons about right behavior. Rarely will a stubborn child learn not to touch a hot stove until he actually experiences the pain of the touch for himself. A wise parent may frequently warn the child of serious consequences, but the willful child will usually find a way to find out for himself. A parent always suffers great pain when her child hurts, but knows that the child has learned not only to respect the dangers of the stove, but that listening and obeying the parent's warnings are important for his safety and his growth.

I stated earlier in the chapter that there was a deep-seated, willful independence in my life that was a serious obstacle to the lordship of Jesus Christ. I was willing to allow God to come along side me and give me everything I wanted. "Bless me, Lord! Just let me run things." We pray "Lord, lead me,"—then expect Him to fall in behind us as we continue with our own plans. Later, when we suffer from our mistakes in judgment, we wonder why He did not stop us. Sometimes, when we do not learn, even from our mistakes, the consequences are deadly. God will persist in His warnings, and will consistently discipline a wayward child, but sometimes the consequences of our actions shape our lives for a lifetime. The account in the Bible of King Saul's impatient and willful disobedience to God's command cost him and his family the throne of Israel (1 Sam. 13:11-14). God told him later

(15:23) that his rebellion was the same as witchcraft in His eyes. God then rejected Saul as king.

As I traveled and spoke to women and teens in many cities and towns over many years, I found that approximately 80 - 90% of the women I encountered were living dull, defeated. . .ho-hum Christian lives. So many actually think that "toughing it out" is all there is in Christianity. This is not God's plan, and He has gone to great lengths in the Bible to teach us how to live victorious, exciting and abundant Christian lives. In the next chapter, titled, "The River of No Return", I will share my own experiences of how God brought me to the place of desiring His lordship in my life more than anything else life could offer.

My stubborn willfulness cost me so much. Like the great London Bridge, built on sand, my own construction crumbled and soon began to show cracks of failure. However, God's loving mercy and grace reached down and lifted me up in forgiveness. His great plan for each of us is to establish our feet on His Rock. . .if we are willing. He then offers us His way across the treacherous rivers toward a life of Victory.

I thank God, that He loves me enough to do whatever it takes to keep me from going my own way! I had so much to learn in those days about my stubborn willfulness—and about my Father's loving hand in my life. I still do.

⋐4⋑

"The Bridge Over
The River of No Return"
— *The Bridge of Victory* —

— Allegory —

A large narrow bridge shrouded in mystery stands in the distance. The path leading to the entrance of the bridge is cluttered with discarded belongings of other travelers who once thought of crossing this unusual bridge.

Instructions written on the span above the entrance forbid the traveler from carrying anything with him across this bridge, causing many to hesitate and even falter at this point. Those that are willing to continue are promised abundance on the other side of the river. Everything in your reason rebels, but the shattering experience of the last bridge causes you to continue, no matter what the cost.

Great pillars rise to support the arches that reach across the distance of the bridge. Suspended from the arches in the distance is a mysterious curtain that glistens like spun gold as it gently moves in

70

the breeze. A strange, yet beautiful peace seems to fill the curtain, beckoning the traveler to "Come!"

Across the foundation of the ancient bridge—chiseled deep in the core—are words that seem to glow like burning coals in their brilliance:

"IF ANY MAN WOULD COME AFTER ME, LET HIM DENY HIMSELF, AND TAKE UP HIS CROSS DAILY, AND FOLLOW ME."[4]

The words are filled with mystery, like a riddle that challenges the traveler to seek its hidden truth. What could this mean? How could anyone die and yet live on the other side of the river?

---

[4] Matthew 16:24, NKJV

"The Bridge Over The River of No Return"

—The Bridge of Victory—

Other than the bridge of salvation, I believe this is one of the most important bridges that a Christian can cross. It is also one of the most difficult. There are others that seem to cause more pain and are certainly more treacherous, but this one involves decisions that can forever change the direction and purpose of the whole journey.

Promises of rewards often cause us to approach this bridge with enthusiasm and interest, until we begin to stumble over the choices that we must make to leave the old life behind.

I can remember, even as a teen, hearing a sermon that spoke to me from the pulpit about the dangers of "sitting on the fence" as Christian young people. The pastor's eyes would search the faces of each of us sitting in the old pews for some flicker of positive response. I was never able to look him in the eye during those sermons because my mind was listing all of the fun things that I was sure that I would have to give up in order to agree to such a drastic measure. I always listened intently with fear and trembling because I knew in my heart that he was right, and that his warnings were for our own good. Still, it always made me uneasy because I understood the difficult choices of being "sold out," so to speak, for Jesus Christ. I listened to him warn about the dangers of compromise, but was sure that I had plenty of time to make this decision at some time in the future. . .perhaps, when I was older.

We have many ideas about the "abundant life" talked about in the Bible (John 10:10b). Even as adult Christians, we secretly feel that we can shop for the parts of that life that are visibly spiritual and easy to wear, without having to make the hard choices that cost us the activities and habits that we enjoy. We think that we can "put on" Christianity like an overcoat that covers the comfortable clothing that we prefer to wear around the house. The Bible says, *"No servant can serve two masters; for either he will hate the one and love the other, or else he will be loyal to the one and despise the other. You cannot serve*

God and mammon" (Luke 16:13). The word, "mammon" here means in the Hebrew, "riches," or "treasure."

As I stated in another chapter, God is committed to growing us up in Jesus Christ. His classroom is always designed to fit our own particular stubbornness and self-will, but can be painfully hard to digest. Even though He warns us in His Word about the dangers of making wrong choices, we still insist on going our own way. This was a hard and painful lesson, but God did not give up on me.

After college I returned to my mother's home in Jackson, Mississippi to teach Science in a local Junior High School. I was soon engaged to a handsome young man that met all of my requirements for excitement and success. As I began to plan my wedding, my life was completely consumed with my own plans, and myself. There was no room left to consider how far away I had pushed Jesus Christ and His plan for my life! I no longer even consulted Him for His direction and care. I think that I knew in my heart that He would not be pleased with my plans—or me, and I did not dare risk His interference. The world offered so many prizes that I wanted and they were all within my reach. "If God would just bear with me until I got all of the important things that I needed, then perhaps we could work things out." The expectations of success for a woman of my day seemed to be like an unwritten schedule that loomed before you like a ticking clock. Though perhaps unspoken, these demands and pressures were real and the need to prove to the world continued to be a prime focus in my life. By now, I had made many wrong choices and did not dare to stop long enough to think about the consequences. I knew that I was far from God, but could not allow myself to stop now. My heart secretly longed for God's fellowship, but I was sure that, after all of His love and blessings in my life, I had committed an unforgivable affront to His love. I was hiding from Him just as Adam and Eve hid from God in the Garden of Eden after their sin.

I remember asking my future husband if he was a Christian and his reply to me was, "Of course!" This was the answer that I wanted to hear. I knew that the Bible said that a Christian must not be *"unequally yoked with an unbeliever"* (2 Cor. 6:14). In the late '50's it was still a social plus to be considered a Christian, therefore, many people really did not know what it meant to be "born again" (John 3:3) in Jesus Christ. Many people in America considered the definition of Christian to mean that they believed that God existed. Most had attended church at some time growing up, and felt that was all that was important. When he responded with his answer that day, I still remember the quiet caution deep in my spirit, but I would not listen, and we were soon married.

Two years later we were transferred to Kansas City where we purchased a home in Overland Park, Kansas. We bought a small house in the suburbs that was framed with beautiful oak trees and a small rock stream running along the back of the lot. The hillside behind the stream was thick with trees and underbrush.

I found the move to this new city a wonderful adventure! The opportunity to teach Health and Physical Education was exciting and I dove into my new task with enthusiasm. A new home in this new city with new beginnings was sure to solve all of my anxiety and I quickly pushed the past worries far into the background.

In February of that year, I found out that I was pregnant with my first little girl and I took a leave of absence from teaching. My little daughter was born in late September and soon became the joy of my life. All of my fears dissolved with this new responsibility that added a wonderful new dimension to my life. Very soon after she was born, I met and became friends with the young woman who lived across the street from me. Sue had a 2 year-old daughter and a brand new baby son and we had great times taking our little ones on walks in their strollers and visiting with each other over coffee. She seemed to have a wealth of information on the ins-and-outs of parenting, which I desperately needed. When the time came for me to return to teaching, I could not bring myself to give up this new thrill of being a *mommy* full-time. I retired from teaching, always with the intention that I would someday return to this wonderful profession.

Next door to me on the left was an older woman whose children were grown. She was a lovely woman who had endured the trauma and pain of breast cancer and the removal of both of her breasts. Just after I met her, the cancer had re-occurred in several places in her body. I had never before known anyone who had suffered so much, physically — and emotionally. Her husband had abandoned her and her three small daughters during the long recovery following the original mastectomies. She shared with Sue and me how she took her three little girls with her to his hotel room and begged him to return to his family. Her persistent prayer and faith in God sustained her through this, and other heartaches of unreal proportions.

Sue and I watched her life in amazement as a quiet peace and beauty always seemed to follow her as she continued with most of her activities. She was always eager to invite us into her lovely country kitchen for coffee and something warm and wonderful, fresh from her oven. Even after her body grew frail and her strength was diminished from the cancer, her beautiful countenance was radiant with the peace of Jesus Christ. On Wednesday mornings, Sue and I would often watch from my front kitchen window, as a group of women would arrive at her house with Bibles tucked under their arms for a Bible study.

Her husband had built a cedar bench around a large oak tree in front of their house and she would sometimes sit there in the shade and read her Bible. As I watched her there, I often remembered the sweet fellowship that I had once known with my Savior and wondered how I had strayed so far away from Him. My life had changed so much from those days at French Camp Academy. The fears and struggles that I had known before Jesus Christ came into my life had now returned and were just as real to me as before. What had happened to move me so far away from Him? Had God abandoned me?

One thing I was sure of, God could never forgive me, now! He had loved me and blessed my life so much, and somehow, I just turned my back on Him and walked away. If I had done so many wonderful things for someone else, and they had turned away from me—I would never speak to them again! I was lonely and ashamed and felt that I must avoid this woman. If she knew, she would want nothing to do with me, either. How could I explain to her what I did not understand myself?

Then one day, I looked out my kitchen window to see Sue sitting on the bench with her. Sue had tears running down her cheeks and I watched as this lovely lady turned from one verse to another in her Bible. As they held hands and prayed together, my heart began to break inside. I knew that in that moment, Sue was being introduced to Jesus Christ. I wanted to run and hide. The feelings in my heart swarmed with confusion. By now, my life bore none of the characteristics of Christianity that I once had known. I was sure that this sweet lady felt that I needed Jesus Christ in my life just as much as Sue.

Sue began attending the Wednesday morning Bible study next door and although she had invited me to come with her, I was determined that I could not bear the scrutiny. Nor did I want to risk having to explain my circumstances, so I retreated into that shell of isolation that had always been a means of protection for me. Sue frequently called on the phone, but I avoided her with many excuses. In June of that year we were blessed with our second little daughter, and my life was full to overflowing. How could I ever be lonely again? But my spiritual emptiness left me hungry inside. God began to bombard my life with a great desire to return to that place of peace and fellowship that I had once known.

The phone rang one morning, and before I could think of an excuse not to talk, Sue invited me to attend a luncheon with her. She bubbled with the description of a fashion show and fun—and a chance to get away from the diapers and runny noses and spend the afternoon with adult women. Oh, it sounded so good! How could I possibly say no? I agreed to go with her to a Christian Women's Club luncheon, and it was as much fun as Sue had said it would be. The women were warm and friendly and many of them reminded me of favorite staff members from college.

At the end of the program, a beautiful white-haired lady with a lovely accent stood up and shared from the Bible. I really was not listening to her words, thinking that I had heard it all so many times before, but in her eyes I saw the love of Jesus Christ. My heart felt the same overwhelming awareness of God's love toward me that I had experienced that decisive evening at French Camp Academy when I heard the message of salvation for the first time. My knees were weak beneath me and I fought to control the tears that wanted to explode within my heart. I was quiet on the way home, except to thank Sue for inviting me to such a beautiful gathering. I knew that, more than anything else in the world, I needed to talk to my Father in heaven and ask Him if He could possibly forgive me. My heart was so homesick for His fellowship that I could barely maintain my composure.

When I arrived home, I paid the baby sitter and busied myself around the house until I put my children down for an afternoon nap. Then I went into the dining room and knelt against a chair and began to weep uncontrollable tears before my Father in Heaven. I felt like the prodigal son in the parable that Jesus had told in Luke 15:11-24. I, too, had wasted my inheritance, and wanted to come home to my heavenly Father. Would He welcome me home as the father in the parable had done? Could He forgive me so much? When I rose from my knees, my face and eyes were swollen, but my heart was free. I had asked Jesus Christ to forgive my sin, and restore me to His fellowship and love.

His forgiving grace flooded my heart. The amazing account of the father's love is explained in the parable:

> *"But the father said to his servants, 'Bring out the best robe and put it on him, and put a ring on his hand and sandals on his feet. And bring the fatted calf here and kill it, and let us eat and be merry; for this my son was dead and is alive again; he was lost and is found'"* (Luke 15:22-24).

In that moment, I knew that I had never ceased to be His child! Yes, I had wandered far from His fellowship, but just as one of my children could never cease to be my child, no matter what they might ever do, neither could I cease to be a child of God! The Bible tells us that God has purchased us with the blood of Jesus Christ (1 Cor. 6:20).

Jesus says in John 10:28-29, *"And I give them eternal life, and they shall never perish; neither shall anyone snatch them out of My hand. My Father, who has given them to Me, is greater than all; and no one is able to snatch them out of My Father's hand."*

In the weeks and months following this encounter with God, I memorized these verses and read them over and over. They have become a major part of the foundation on which the remainder of my life with Jesus Christ has been built.

—The Hopeless Struggle—

Soon after that, I shared with Sue and the lady next door how God had used each of them to make me desperately hungry to be restored to my Father's fellowship. I began attending the Christian Women's Club meetings on a regular basis and signed up to participate in their Bible correspondence course. I remember how I loved to receive their weekly lessons. Every day, while my little girls napped in the afternoon, I would take out my lessons and turn in the Scriptures to find the answers. Yes, I had studied so much of the Bible before, but this was different. Now, I devoured every word like a starving child! Every passage I read was beautiful and exciting, and I could not get enough! I attended prayer seminars and learned to pray conversationally. This prayer seminar transformed my thinking about talking and listening to God on an intimate new level. My prayer time with Him became personal and real instead of dutiful and orchestrated by memorized words. I learned that I could converse with God as I walked on the street or through the house.

I knew that I had received the wonderful gift of salvation that night when I was 15, but now, I was in love with Jesus Christ! My heart was filled with wanting to know Him and a genuine desire to please Him! I realized now that the world with all of its glitter and promise was nothing but emptiness and fading promises to one who had once tasted the sweetness of God's presence!

As my life began to change, all of my appetites began to change. My husband was more than a little stunned at this *new person* who had replaced the one he had married. I thought that he would be pleased, but this was not the case. Then, one day, I found a verse in the Bible that explained to me why some people who do not know Jesus Christ are uncomfortable around Christians. *"For we are to God the fragrance of Christ among those who are being saved and among those who are perishing. To the one we are the aroma of death leading to death, and to the other the aroma of life leading to life"* (2 Cor. 2:15-16). In other words, the aroma of Jesus Christ in a life makes an unbeliever aware of his or her own state of spiritual death. I began to pray fervently for my husband's salvation.

Through Sue's new Christian friends, I was also exposed to leaders in the Campus Crusade for Christ ministry and began to attend some of their evangelism seminars. I learned how to share my testimony with others and how to explain so much about my faith. These truths were very valuable in helping me understand what had happened to me in college. Their little booklets showed me that when Jesus Christ comes into a heart, He takes His place on the throne of that heart. They explained, very simply and effectively, that Jesus Christ would not share His place on the throne of a life! Either He will be on that throne as Lord of your life, or, if you choose, *you* will occupy that place of control of your own life. A born again Christian that has taken control of running his own life; one that has either knowingly or unknowingly, abandoned the Lordship of Jesus Christ in his life, is what the apostle Paul describes in one of his letters to the church at Corinth as worldly, or "carnal."

"And I, brethren, could not speak to you as to
spiritual people but as to carnal, as to babes in Christ.

I fed you with milk and not with solid food; for until now you were not able to receive it, and even now you are still not able; for you are still carnal. For where there are envy, strife, and divisions among you, are you not carnal and behaving like mere men?" 1 Cor. 3:1-3).

This was and is a fascinating explanation of why I could be a born-again Christian. . .and still be so tied to the world. I had never grown-up as a Christian!

As my college career had progressed, without knowing what I was doing in the spiritual realm, I had taken over control of my life and usurped Jesus' place as Lord of my life! I had busily gone about furthering my own agenda, rather than seeking God's direction for my life. I became once again, lord of my own life, just as I had been before I met Him. Only now, there was severe conflict in my heart, because now there were two masters in my life.

Another passage that explained this conflict that was going on in my life was Galatians. 5:17, *"For the flesh lusts against the Spirit, and the Spirit against the flesh; and these are contrary to one another, so that you do not do the things that you wish."*

— Civil War —

Civil war had broken out in my heart, and I did not understand what had happened to me. Yes, I was still a Christian, but unless Jesus Christ is in control, all of the characteristics; the fears and pain of a life without Christ begin to invade your life once again. No wonder I had been so miserable! I did not want this to happen again and I poured myself into reading and understanding God's Word.

I also began attending a neighborhood Bible class taught by a Christian woman whose husband was involved in the lay ministry of Campus Crusade for Christ. Jan was probably the most radiant Christian woman I have ever known. When she taught the Bible, women sat in corners and on the floor to listen and learn. I could not put my finger on the special ingredient that she possessed, but I was sure that I wanted it! Love and sincerity literally oozed from her heart and eyes. As I studied and prayed to be all that God wanted me to be, I was sure that all I had to do was mimic Jan. But the harder I tried, the more I failed. I read in the Bible so many things that I just could not accomplish, like 1 John 4:20, 21. There were other Christians that I just could not stand! This troubled me a great deal. I would smile at them in an insincere honey-coated sort of way, but it always made me sick to my stomach. I had been exposed to so many over-sweet Christian types that seemed fake and empty to me and I could not settle for that in my life. There was also much scripture about lying and gossip and anger. My impatience and anger with others especially concerned me for I knew that Jesus would never be impatient with others or angry over such insignificant things.

It seemed that the more I tried, the more I failed to be all that the Bible said I should be as a Christian woman. In the past, the achievement of success had always meant that I must try harder! Why did this prize seem to slip through my fingers like wisps of smoke? I would pray with all of my heart for God to change me, but then I only seemed to get worse. I felt like such a hopeless hypocrite inside! What was wrong with me?

The struggle became more and more difficult and I grew very frustrated with my failure to live this Christian life! Every time I went to Jan's Bible study and watched and listened to this beautiful woman, I grew more and more discouraged with my efforts. Then one evening, alone in my dining room, I dropped to my knees weeping and praying to my Father about my failures.

The Christian life was not only difficult—**it was impossible!**

I was sure that I could not be the person that God wanted me to be! I wanted so much to be pleasing to God in every part of my life! I went to bed that night resolving to only attend Jan's class one last time. It had grown increasingly difficult to be around these godly women with their sweet and forgiving smiles and their perfect loving ways. If I could not be like them, I certainly did not want to watch them! My heart was filled with sadness as I closed my eyes and cried myself to sleep.

I arrived at the Bible study among the crowd of women, and found myself a spot on the floor in a secluded corner of the room. Jan opened with her usual soft prayer that always made me feel as though everyone else in the room was eavesdropping on an intimate conversation between her and God.

When she finished, she reached over and picked up a book lying on the table next to her. Then she held the book up for everyone to see and said that God had shown her that there might be someone in the class who was having difficulty *living* the Christian life.

"If so," she said, "I brought this book that might help you understand."

— <u>Magnificent Revelation</u> —

I jumped from my corner and sailed across the bodies jammed into every open spot in the room. Within moments, I had returned to my place and began reading Watchman Nee's book, "The Normal Christian Life."[5] From that moment on, I was oblivious to everyone and everything else in the room.

When the class was over, I hurried home and quickly fed my little girls their lunch. Finally, when I tucked them in for their naps, I sat in the dining room chair that had become my study place, and began to devour this book. It was as if Watchman Nee had written this book just for me. Jan had been teaching on the book of Romans and had said so many things that I now read in the first chapter of Watchman Nee's book, but somehow there seemed to be a new ingredient. I would realize later that this new ingredient was quite possibly that my heart was now ready to agree with God about my **inability** to be all that Jesus wanted to be in my heart!

I had finally discovered that I just could not be good enough! Watchman Nee explained that no one could live the Christian life within his or her self. The only way to live for Christ was to **die to self**. I learned that the old sin nature that each of us inherited from our father, Adam, cannot be cleaned up—it must die on the cross with Jesus Christ. . . but, how?

This really does not make any sense to the reasoning mind. He explained that no matter how hard you struggle to understand this on your own, you could not figure it out. He said that the Holy Spirit of God must reveal these truths to a person's heart! The Bible says, *"I have been crucified with Christ; it is no longer I who live, but Christ lives in me; and the life which I now live in the flesh I live by faith in the Son of God, who loved me and gave Himself for me"* (Gal. 2:20). The apostle Paul calls this ***"the mystery hidden from the ages and***

---

[5] The Normal Christian Life, by Watchman Nee. Christian Literature Crusade, Montreal, Quebec. © 1961 Angus I. Kinnear.

from generations, but now has been revealed to His saints . . .which is Christ in you, the hope of glory" (Col. 1:26-27).

He clearly explained that this verse proved that the wonderful work of *making me holy* had already been accomplished at Calvary! Such confusion! I was more than aware of my failure to live and walk in holiness before God! Perhaps it had just not worked for me—**maybe I really was an impossible case!**

I learned that a Christian no longer had to struggle to be good because the "power of sin" over our lives had been broken by the death and resurrection of Jesus Christ on the cross at Calvary. It had already been accomplished for me, but I had to accept it—by faith!

This is a mystery of God. **Our own reasoning cannot figure it out!** The best part is that He **wants** to reveal these mysteries to His children! I understood that I needed to ask God to give me understanding. I was beginning to see the reason for the confusion and conflict that I had gone through in college. These chapters in the Bible were surely written just for me (Rom. 6 & 7). It all sounded wonderful, but how could anyone put all of this into practice? Heaven knows I tried!—And tried—and tried! But, as I read from Watchman Nee's book that day, I knew that my Father planned to show me this wonderful truth. I slipped quietly to my knees and began to pray. . .

"Father in heaven, I cannot do it myself! I ask You to give me a revelation that will show me how to live 'in Christ.' I no longer want to live as a hypocrite. I would rather have you take my life than to go on living a life that dishonors your name."

I have never found words to describe what happened next. There were no visible angels in the room, although I am sure that they were singing the Hallelujah chorus in heaven.

"Hallelujah, she has found out that she cannot do it herself!"

But in that moment, a quiet **knowing** dropped into my heart as the Holy Spirit opened my heart to His truth.

God seemed to draw back a spiritual curtain and reveal to my heart the truth of these mysteries that I read before, but could not understand. I could not move as I felt the personal presence of my Savior all around me. I knew that He was there, and I knew that I would never be the same again. I stayed in that place for as long as my knees would bear me, weeping in His presence.

The Bible tells us that God has chosen to reveal these mysteries of His kingdom to you and to me (Matt. 13:10-11). But, until I reached the point that I wanted Jesus Christ to run my life unconditionally—until I really saw my own botched efforts and chose to give them up, I was not truly ready for Him to be "Lord of my life". Paul explains this mystery further in his letter to the church at Colossia: *". . .the mystery which has been hidden from ages and from generations, but now has been revealed to His saints. To them God willed to make known what are the riches of the glory of this mystery among the Gentiles: which is Christ in you, the hope of glory."* (Col. 1:26-27).

This is still almost incomprehensible to me. No one on earth could have been less deserving than I was. But, the Bible says that because I am now *"in Christ,"* the fullness of God now lives within me (Col. 2:9-11)! Wow! It is a magnificent miracle, indeed, how the great God of the universe, could love someone so undeserving as me enough to reveal Himself in my heart. But, as I would learn from His Word, this wonderful gift is not based on me; it is based on His Son Jesus Christ and the value that God the Father places on His blood that was poured out at Calvary! God has chosen to reveal His mysteries, hidden since the beginning of time, to those who trust in Him.

When I finally returned to the chair that day, I continued reading from Watchman Nee's book with new understanding of his words. He explained that I must die to my right to run my own life and that this would not happen until I was ready to come to the end of myself. This is why I had failed so miserably—I stubbornly insisted in my heart that **I could do it!** God was answering my prayer to be completely His. My stubborn independence and reliance upon **my** abilities would never allow Him to be Lord. I needed to come to the place where I no longer wanted **me** as Lord of my life!

As I write this, I am reminded of another woman who discovered this great mystery at a conference at Glen Eyrie, Colorado, a conference grounds just outside of Colorado Springs. I was speaking on this same subject. When this revelation dropped from her head into her heart, she jumped to her feet and ran from the room. Before the meeting was over, she returned to her chair with her eyes shining. She later told me that her father was a minister and they had both been puzzled all of their Christian lives by the *impossible* task of trying to live the way God wanted them to in the Bible. She said that she walked down the aisle of her church almost every Sunday morning to renew her commitment to Jesus Christ, but she never felt the assurance that she knew she was supposed to have. When she ran from the room, she ran to call her father to tell him that she now had the answer, for both of them! She said that she just could not wait to tell him that they could both finally stop struggling—Jesus Christ had already accomplished it all for them! The Christian life, from start to finish, is a story of freedom, but so many never discover this truth that will usher them into victory and power in Jesus Christ. This is what you would truly call a "life and death issue." This wonderful abundant life of victory and freedom in Jesus Christ requires death—a willingness to die to your own rights to be Lord of your life, moment by moment! Jesus spoke of this mystery before His death,

> *"Most assuredly, I say to you, unless a grain of wheat falls into the ground and dies, it remains alone; but if it dies, it produces much grain. He who loves his life will lose it, and he who hates his life in this world will keep it for eternal life"* (John 12:24-25).

Jack Taylor, in his wonderful book, The Key to Triumphant Living[6], explains this great mystery simply and beautifully. I found his book to be a valuable tool when teaching women's retreats on this subject. It shares his own testimony of how God brought him to the end of his stubborn insistence on "doing it his way," to the revelation in his heart of "Christ in you, the hope of glory."

A few years later, as women began to wrestle with the feminine movement's concern over the identity issue; many women became concerned with this Biblical concept of "dying to self." After all, the new rallying cry for women was to "be who you are!" To "die to self" implied that a Christian woman must be a sort of, mousy—door-mat nobody! Nothing could be further from the truth. The Bible tells us that God created each of us with a unique purpose and plan. The real problem is that until we are "re-created in Jesus Christ" (Eph. 9:10), we are not free to be His unique design (Psalm 139:14-16). I believe it is like buying a rose bush that has all of the wonderful properties within its roots to be a magnificent producer of exquisite blooms. However, until it is planted in the rich soil of God's life giving nourishment; it is just a barren plant resting among all of the other barren plants at the

---

[6] The Key To Triumphant Living, by Jack Taylor. Broadman Press, Nashville TN. © 1971, Broadman Press.

nursery. I have watched many, many women whose lives were gray and empty before they met Jesus Christ, and I have seen those lives break forth in strength and beauty through the inner working of His life within them.

With this new understanding, I was obnoxious with excitement over new freedom in Jesus Christ! I no longer struggled to be like *Jesus* because I had been shown by the Holy Spirit that **I cannot be like Jesus—only Jesus living in me can be like Jesus!** I learned that as I chose to lay down my scepter of rule, daily—moment by moment, I began to experience His magnificent life of freedom within my heart! This was not an easy task!

This magnificent truth was not new. Paul had gone to great lengths to teach it to the early churches. His letters from Rome go to great lengths to teach the early Christians this mystery of how to live and walk in victory (Rom. 7 & 8). The "fly in the ointment" is that our sin nature, sometimes referred to in the Bible as the flesh, will do just about anything to keep from giving up control of our lives. Contrary to what we may believe, it does not go away at the moment of salvation. **It cannot be cleaned up or reformed!** The only solution for it is death. It must be nailed to the cross with Jesus. It will go to Sunday school, attend church regularly, even preach and teach. . .as long as it does not have to die.

— Four Basic Steps to Victory —

There are four basic steps that I learned by going through this process of learning to walk in victory with Christ. God had already taken me through a painful revelation about myself. I needed to see who I really was without God's lordship in my life. God let me see that without Him in control, I was like a ship on the rocks.

1. Desire the Lordship of Jesus Christ

He made me hungry and thirsty for Jesus (Isa. 44:3). I began to *desire* the Lordship of Jesus in my life. Once I tasted His fellowship in my life as a "new Christian", the world's best was empty and meaningless without Him. Ask Him to give you this desire!

2. <u>Agree</u> with Him

We have to be willing to see our heart the way God sees it. My failure to be all that He described in His Word as a Christian caused me to **agree** with Him about needing to relinquish control of my life to Him. (Rom. 7:18)

3. <u>Reckon</u> yourself "dead to sin"

God then showed me in His Word and through others that I must **"reckon** myself "dead to sin and alive to Jesus Christ" (Rom. 6:11, Gal. 2:20). The word, reckon, means to consider it, or to put faith to the truth! This is first a **choice**. We must make a decision to believe that if God says it in His Word, we have made a decisive choice to consider it as settled fact and from that moment on there is no longer room for doubt.

4. <u>Obey</u>

Then, we **obey**. (James 1:22-24) This is a moment by moment decision. As we obey, we become transformed into the image of Jesus Christ (Rom. 8:29).

❧ ❧ ❧ ❧ ❧ ❧ ❧ ❧ ❧ ❧ ❧

As long as I am willing to give up my rights to live my own way, Jesus will live through me to give me victory over my self-centered will. For the first time in my Christian life, I actually began to experience the victorious Christian life! I had the power to deny my desires to lie and gossip. No, I was not suddenly perfect—far from it! But, now I had the power to choose victory through the denial of my own way, which is powerless to behave the way Christ would behave! I was able to look at people that I did not like and *choose* to love them with the love of Jesus! This was such a miracle to me! Yes, it was still a struggle to choose to allow Him to control my life! My sin nature will struggle to resist and will not go down without dying, as Paul says in Romans 6 and 7. God tells us in Jeremiah that, *"The heart is deceitful above all things, and desperately wicked; who can know it?"* (Jer. 17:9).

— **Demonstration of the Mystery** —

When God teaches us a new and great truth about His kingdom, He often follows with a demonstration in our lives to cement it in our hearts. An example of this new truth happened not long after my new revelation. I lay in bed alone one night deeply concerned about a personal issue between my husband and myself. He had gone out for a late night of bowling with his friends. Things had not been going well in our marriage and I was growing more and more concerned about our future. The smell of alcohol mixed with cheap perfume permeated the room as he climbed into bed and collapsed in sleep. I slipped out of bed and went into the kitchen. I stood there for a long time in the darkness and wept quietly in despair. Finally, Watchman Nee's words from his book vibrated in my ears and I began to whisper a prayer out loud to my Father in heaven: *"Father, if this is all true, I choose to die right now to my right to despise my husband. I choose to give it up to you. If this is really possible, I ask you to fill my heart with your supernatural love for him right now!"*

An incredible miracle happened in the deepest part of my being! Suddenly, my heart was filled with the very love of God for my husband. I had never known anything like this before, nor could I have ever mustered this kind of love for anyone—even someone who I thought might deserve my love. I saw and felt, for the first time, just a small part of the amazing love that my Savior must have felt when He looked down through eternity and saw me in need of that love. I stood there breathless in the darkness for a long time with chills of amazement running through my spirit. I knew that this was that great *mystery of the ages* that Jesus came to reveal to His children, *". . .Christ in you, the hope of glory!"* (Col. 1:27b). God had performed the impossible in my heart—once again!

I returned to the bedroom to find my husband asleep and unaware of the magnificent encounter I had experienced in the kitchen. I lay awake most of the night marveling at this wonderful God who loved us so much to provide such a thrilling and rewarding life for those who choose Him as Lord!

There began to be daily incidents in this struggle to relinquish my rights to run my own life, my way, but when I did make this choice the outcome was amazing to me! No, I did not say it was easy. It was a terrible struggle and one I did not always win! I learned that the old nature of sin and selfishness will dig in its heels and even masquerade as sweetness and light to keep from dying!

I remember an incident that happened in a beauty shop a few years later that really blew me away! When my oldest daughter read the manuscript for this chapter, she said, "Mom, you must not say "beauty shop," any more. It dates you!

I had an orthodox Jewish girl as my hairdresser and she had demonstrated an interest in hearing about Jesus and His claims of being the Messiah. Each time I arrived for my hair appointment, the questions began, and usually continued for the whole time I was there. There was a lady sitting at the next station who, unknown to me, had become very agitated with the conversation that occurred each week. Another lady who attended at the same time had walked over to me and asked me if I had another one of the lovely booklets that I had given her the week before that explained the message of salvation. As I reached into my purse to find one for her, the lady sitting in the chair next to mine, said with a loud and piercing voice,

"Well, I see you are still spouting your little messages to everyone in the shop!"

I was embarrassed and, more than a little irritated by her loud sarcastic condemnation of my efforts to touch the lives of the other women. My thoughts exploded inside my head, and I was so stunned that I could not speak! No one had dared speak to me with such venom since my early days at French Camp Academy. All eyes in the shop were frozen on me to see what I would say to her. I searched for the right words to defend myself. I do not know how long the moment lasted—probably only a microsecond.

At that moment God interrupted my defensive attitude with a question straight to my heart, "Will you allow Jesus to love her?" (Well, this was clearly not my first choice. . .)

We are in such a habit of response in daily encounters with others that we usually shoot first and forget to ask questions later! As I had begun to practice this choice of giving up my own rights, I was beginning to learn the habit of asking God to show me His heart. **The victory is God's, but the choice to die to your own rights—in that moment—swings open the door to His power.** My heart began to soften with the love of Jesus Christ for her, and through God's grace and love, I saw past her words to the heart of pain that she had stuffed way down inside. This one had become very successful at masking her heartache behind angry words.

I turned to her, now with the love of Jesus Christ in my heart and eyes and said, "I have one more of these booklets. Would you like to have it?"

The pause in her response seemed like an eternity. Then with uncontrollable tears in her eyes, she reached out her hand and gently took the little booklet that I held out to her. As I turned my attention again to my hairdresser, I was very aware out of the corner of my eye, that she spent the rest of her time in the chair, devouring the words in the little book that I had given to her. My heart was overwhelmed with the love of Jesus for her! I did not want to think of the different outcome—for her and for me, if I had failed to respond to the nudging of the Holy Spirit in that eternal moment of destiny! This is the difference in the way Jesus responds, and the way I would respond. My rights would have chosen to put her in her place, or at least snub her proving to her probably once again that there is really nothing different in a Christian than anybody else.

There is another experience that I must share about this mystery of loving with the love of Jesus Christ. I call it Calvary Love because it is the same love that reached down from the cross and loved and forgave me when I deserved only judgment for my sin.

A group of dignitaries from my husband's company from the east coast had notified my husband that they would be in town and wanted to take us, and other company people living in Kansas City, out for a night of dinner and entertainment. As the evening approached, I was told that after dinner at a well-known steak house we would all go to a local nightclub that had a particularly disgraceful reputation. I was horrified and embarrassed, and even stunned that my husband would ask me to accompany him to such an immoral place. He was angry at my reaction and insistent that it would be very embarrassing for him if I refused. How would it look to the other couples and his management if I was the only wife that was not there? After a great deal of struggle, I decided that if I refused to go, I might "win a battle, but lose the war," so to speak, with my husband. I knew that God could and would protect me. By now, I understood what God said in His Word to me about being careful to submit to my husband as "my spiritual head" (Eph. 5:22) even though I knew in my heart that he was not a Christian. I had been studying from Shirley Rice's book on "The

Christian Home"[7] and had asked God to teach me how to be the kind of Christian wife and mother that He wanted me to be.

Still, the questions and objections swirled in my thoughts. What if someone saw me there? What kind of witness would this be to them?

These, and other questions plagued me as the day approached, but I comforted myself with the reminder that Jesus was often ridiculed for dining with sinners (Matt. 9:10-13). When the night arrived, our party was seated at a round table in a dimly lighted smoke-filled room of the nightclub that seemed to resemble a large warehouse. The cigarette smoke was stifling and assaulted my nose and eyes so bad that I could barely breathe. The noise in the room was deafening and prohibited any conversation lower than a shout. As I looked around, I noticed that in the center of the room there was a square boxing arena with ropes surrounding the stage. Leading off to the rear of the large room from the stage was a runway that led to a doorway in the back.

Suddenly, there was a loud drum roll and the spot lights centered on this doorway. An enormously large and obese man appeared and as the music began to play, he started to dance his way down the runway toward the stage in the center of the room. As he danced, he began removing his clothing and I realized that he was performing a "strip-tease." The crowd in the room screamed with pleasure at his brazen and raucous behavior. I was horrified! I dropped my head in disgust and shame—shame for him and humiliation for myself that I was there. My next emotion was anger toward my husband for bringing me to this place. It was now evident to me that, not only had he been here before, but also he had been the one to suggest this place to the men who came to town.

Although angry and humiliated, I began to whisper a prayer that had become a habit in my life when faced with difficult people and situations that I knew were impossible for me to handle: "Father, what do You want my attitude to be, right now?"

Once again, the Holy Spirit spoke so clearly to my spirit that it seemed almost audible,

"If he was the only person in the whole world, I still would die for him!"

---

[7] The Christian Home: A Woman's View, by Shirley Rice. Norfolk Christian Schools, Norfolk TN © 1965.

Suddenly, my heart was broken with shame at my attitude toward this man on the stage. As I raised my eyes to look at him, I was able to see him with the eyes of Jesus as He looked down from the cross, and I felt that matchless love pass through my heart! *In one microsecond, God changed my perspective.* How could I reject one that my Savior loved so deeply? As the tears ran down my cheeks, I truly longed for this man to know Jesus Christ. Perhaps he had no one else in the world to care for him enough to ask God for his salvation—but now I loved him with my Savior's love.

At this point, someone in the group suggested that we should leave. As we gathered our things, I knew that God had used another impossible situation to change my heart in a new way. I would never forget the man in the boxing arena and each time I remembered him, I would pray for his salvation and wonder if I will see him again in heaven. I had once again experienced another valuable lesson of God's matchless love for those He died to save!

This incredible Calvary Love reaches into the deepest corner of a heart and imparts love and healing. As it passes through the heart, it leaves in its path, a sheath of light and beauty that changes us forever. It is as far beyond the scope of human explanation as light is from darkness and it cannot be counterfeited—or duplicated apart from Jesus Christ.

So often, the traveler hesitates to cross this mysterious bridge. The promises of abundance on the other side of the river are often overlooked in the struggle to carry baggage with you across the bridge. At the time, the cost of leaving so much behind seems painful and even impossible to bear, but then as you look back, the treasures of the world that were once so important, now appear as only rubbish from the other side of the river.

> *"Yet indeed I also count all things loss for the excellence of the knowledge of Christ Jesus my Lord, for whom I have suffered the loss of all things, and count them as rubbish, that I may gain Christ. . ."*
> (Phil. 3:8-9).

"A Bridge Too Far"

— The Bridge of Forgiveness —

— Allegory —

T he beauty of the hills has now mystically faded into a shadowy wasteland where barren campsites dot the countryside. Travelers stooped with heavy burdens seem to have stumbled and lost their way as they approach the entrance to the next bridge.

The full span of this old bridge with its beams and girders rests on one great cornerstone with ancient words chiseled deep within the stone at its base. These words seem to echo a warning to those seeking to pass. Beyond the entrance, the interior is shrouded in secrets with the movement of lights and shadows that produce an eerie sense of mystery.

Whispers can now be heard from the shadows within the covered entrance of the bridge adding to its mystery. A large door, battered by the onslaught of many angry storms, now fills the dark corridor, blocking passage to the other side. This dark door with its rusty old hinges that rattle and creak in the wind seems somehow familiar, yet impenetrable, to the one who stands before it. Heavy chains and locks prohibit passage for one seeking to leave this darkness behind.

Your attention is somehow drawn to the golden key placed in your hand at the great Golden Gate and your heart begins to pound with awareness of the choice before you. You know that the key will open the locks and loose the chains, but emotions and fears paralyze the heart. What terrible heaviness hinders you from placing the key in the lock that will open this door? As your eyes begin to focus in the shadows, some pain deep within you reminds you that you, yourself hammered out the locks and placed them on the gate. Each ugly lock on the old door came at great cost to you and reminds you of the bitter reasons for placing them there.

Could there be another way around this bridge? Even as the question forms in your heart, you remember the campsites along the path leading to the bridge's entrance. Familiar voices can now be heard reminding you of your rights. No one can make you cross this bridge.

As you pause before the door, you realize that you must carefully weigh the cost of giving up your rights to harbor and cherish your own familiar pain. Beams of light begin to flicker through the cracks in the old door revealing the warmth of freedom on the other side. The flickering light that falls across your heart begins to make you aware of the Master Builder's presence with you in the darkness.

Remembrance of the warning chiseled on the cornerstone of the bridge reminds you of the urgency to place the key in the large lock that will open the door. Your trembling heart somehow knows that the choice is yours. As you turn to seek His help, the scars in His hands remind you of the great cost to Him in building this bridge of forgiveness. Finally, as you surrender the key into His hand, the door swings open as though anticipating His touch. Suddenly you find yourself experiencing the warmth and freedom of the sunshine on the other side of the bridge.

"A Bridge Too Far"

— *The Bridge of Forgiveness* —

There are many difficult roadblocks that confront us on this journey, but none more subtle; none more hazardous, than those that we encounter on the road to forgiveness. Forgiveness is the work of the Cross and Jesus makes it indelibly clear that we cannot follow Him in this journey unless we, too, take up this work of the cross.

Un-forgiveness has at its core the very sin nature that Jesus died to defeat in our lives. It becomes the sin nature's "ace in the hole" within the heart and will keep us confused and powerless to be all that God wants us to be.

We seem to have defense mechanisms that give each of us a justifiable right to make this the exception to the rule of Christianity. The sin nature that we inherited from Adam does not go away just because we accept Jesus Christ as Savior. Un-forgiveness claims rights and privileges that want to supersede God's commands, when, in fact, it is just the opposite. Forgiveness is the most basic work of grace that the cross of Jesus Christ offers to us.

We seem to see clearly how others should apply forgiveness in their relationships, but when it comes to our own private pain, we are likely to soothe our wounded heart with the excuse that "no one understands." There are some that we easily work through, but the deep hurts are often tucked away in a private place for future visitation. Some are so painful that we cannot even bear to remember them, lest they rise up like a monster from our past to destroy us.

Some of us may even think that this is not an issue for us. We sometimes feel that we really do not have any feelings of un-forgiveness toward anyone. And then, when something happens that triggers a hurtful memory of how someone has unjustly wronged us, we find ourselves angry and tearful inside. It is like an old dusty recording that slips off the shelf and begins to play in the heart. Its tune takes us into the hurts so vividly that we are powerless to hear much else.

How do we deal with something so painful to the touch? Most of us choose not to. We think that the old saying, "time heals all wounds" will eventually erase the memory and the pain, but it cannot. This is only an attempt to avoid facing the real issue; the issue that we must forgive others as Jesus forgave us; unconditionally and completely.

We are bewildered when we use the old tried and tried again formulas for forgiveness. We often think that a sincere "saying it," is all that is needed. I can remember my little girl tossing her head with that twinkle in her eye, followed by a sweet and contrite, "Sorry, Mom." This was supposed to erase the offense from my mind and remove the fear of consequences from hers. The old nature comes prepared even in the youngest and cutest packages, does it not? Only forgiveness will heal and restore the heart and spirit—not time, or careless words that we throw at the problem. God provides the answer, and only His answer will erase the barriers and locks that an offense will build around the heart. Un-forgiveness will scar the Christian spirit and keep us forever dwelling in a wasteland of bitterness and resentment. This is serious business, indeed, and God's warnings are very clear for the Christian.

Jesus Christ came to forgive and heal the heart of man. He will not accept a cover-up, or our own version of the rules. He is not only our example of forgiveness, but **He provides the power within our heart to make it happen.** The Bible says that His strength and power is made perfect in our weakness (2 Cor. 12:9). If we insist on withholding forgiveness toward someone until they have earned it, we may be locking ourselves in a sad and bitter box for a lifetime. We will be the one who suffers over and over. . .and over again. I have even talked to women that have difficulty remembering what really happened. All they really remember is the pain that the offense has left in the heart, and that their rights have been violated. This has destroyed families and relationships down through the centuries. Countries have fought wars and destroyed nations to prove that they were right.

When we meet Jesus Christ at Calvary we usually feel that this problem with the past will be somehow, miraculously erased. What we usually do not realize is that He has placed the keys of forgiveness in our hands. We have to be the one that unlocks the chains and barriers that we have learned to jealously guard.

— <u>Power to Choose to Obey</u> —

When God finally got my attention by shining a spotlight on this very serious issue in my life, I found that my old attitude of self-fixit just would not work. This was far too serious. In fact, the cords of un-forgiveness were wound so tightly around my heart that I was completely powerless to even face them without the love and gentle touch of Jesus and His intervention. I did not want to be responsible for dealing with the pain of the past. I wanted God to send me through His spiritual car wash and make me come out perfect on the other side.

It seems that in my own life I had so many serious things to learn that I barely got through one mine-field and I would find myself right in the middle of another one! I would soon learn, though, that Christianity is a *process* that we must "grow through." It is not a one-time event! As I began to grow in this new awareness of "Christ in you, the hope of glory," my feet barely touched the ground in the joy of my new perspective.

But as the weeks passed, I found that there were still bridges to be crossed. I discovered that the old sin nature still must be kept on the cross **daily**. Then I began to discover that because of the deep hurts of the past, there were still rooms hidden away in the recesses of my heart that I had refused to open. I had given Jesus all of the title deed to my life, except this protected and locked cellar that I had marked "Do Not Enter!"

I had not realized the depth of un-forgiveness in my heart until my mom came to visit me following the birth of my first little girl. I had asked her to come and help me with the new baby, and I could tell that she was more than pleased at the invitation. Although I was thrilled to have her there to rescue me from this mountain of bottles and diapers and this adorable little interruption to my organized life, I became aware of feelings inside me that I had hidden for most of my life. Each time she tried to hug me, my skin crawled at her touch and I recoiled and pushed her away. She was deeply hurt by my reaction and I hated seeing the pain in her eyes. Why had these deep feelings of resentment toward her, hidden away all of these years, suddenly surfaced now? Why couldn't I bear her touch? I was deeply puzzled by the fact that this business of forgiveness was not just automatically taken care of when I experienced the life changing victory of being "in Christ." How could I have tasted the sweet presence of the in-dwelling power and freedom that comes with knowing my Savior in such a powerful and intimate way, and still be lacking in anything?

After she left to return home, I once again put the whole problem out of my mind. I had learned years ago to successfully manage these unmanageable problems of pain by pushing them into some hidden part of my mind someplace, so that I would not have to deal with them.

Two years later when she came to see us after I had turned my life back over to Jesus Christ, I thought that it would be different, but it was not. I tried to pretend affection toward her, but felt like a hypocrite inside. I knew that she was not fooled and I grieved over my response toward her. My renewed commitment to Jesus Christ was foremost in my heart and I wanted desperately to please Him in every part of life. I knew what the Bible said about forgiveness and Jesus' warnings about refusing to forgive (Matt. 6:14-15), but, how?

Would any kind of remorse on my mother's part ever be enough to blot out the memories of the separation and rejection that I felt as a child?

How could I ever erase the lonely memories of my ten year-old heart, alone night after night in the little bunk in the darkness?

Would my dad ever be able to restore the lack of caring and concern that I had missed and so desperately needed from him?

Would my stepmother be able to make up for the theft of my father's love that was snatched away from our home?

Would I ever be able to face the sadness of these memories and forgive the way Jesus wanted me to? Was I supposed to just wipe the slate clean and pretend that none of the pain happened?

These and other questions had been hidden away deep in my heart with the intention of never facing them because the answers could possibly be worse than the questions. My way of coping with these memories of the past had always been avoidance, and I had become very good at avoiding any kind of tender encounter with those that had hurt me so deeply.

My reaction toward my mother still stunned me. Yes, I did love her, but why couldn't I stand for her to touch me? I knew that she loved me deeply and would obviously sacrifice her own life for me. I wanted to show love to her, but something within me could not!

It was like a terrible storm that confronted me when we were together. I could see the darkness of the cloud that engulfed me, but refused the shelter that was always visible for entrance. The handle to open the door to the shelter was there, but I could not bring myself to reach for it. I found myself aloof to the damage of the storm that it seemed to bring in my mother's heart. I despised this in me, but how could I face these shadows that had been hidden for so long? I felt that if I opened my heart to the pain, all of the ugly memories would escape like monsters from Pandora's Box and I would forever be lost in the unhappiness of the past. The strong survival instinct that I had nurtured since childhood demanded that the only solution for peace and happiness was to keep them deeply and forever hidden. Wasn't this the best solution? When Jesus Christ touched my life, His supernatural love seemed to draw back a curtain of hope for a future life of normalcy. If I allowed the pain of the past to raise its ugliness again, would I lose the wonderful life I had found? Rejection had torn at my child's heart so completely that self-worth had been shredded into a thousand pieces. As a result, the ability to receive and accept love had become **conditional** based on performance and/or achievement.

No wonder I had been so driven in college. Even though I did not really know why, I had a learned response that my peers and professors could only accept me if I proved my worth to them through outstanding achievement. When I worked so hard to prove my qualifications for the student position I sought for my senior year, and failed anyway, I was confused and devastated. When Jesus Christ came into my heart at 15, He had shown me that His love was not conditional. In fact, His love was a free gift, and could never be connected to anything I might ever **be** or **do**. This was like being set free from a battle that I could never win, or a prison that I could never escape! I had never known this kind of acceptance and love before. Even though I believed completely that He loved me, I still had a long road ahead in applying this love and acceptance to the rest of my life. Yes, God loved me freely and unconditionally, but I still could not believe that the rest of the world could accept me in such a way.

After that wonderful day when I knelt and asked Jesus to forgive me and restore my fellowship with Him, I really expected all of those shadows of hurt and pain in my life to disappear, but they did not. I still felt warped inside. I knew that this un-forgiveness would destroy the beauty of my walk with Jesus Christ if I did not lay it down. I wanted to be able to give my mother the love that she deserved, but I found that it was just not that easy for me. I just could not fake it. I read all that the Bible said about forgiveness and the warnings connected to this terrible sin of un-forgiveness, and it terrified me! I realized that it would be dangerous, indeed, for me to ignore them.

— Un-forgiveness Hinders Effective Prayer —

Jesus gives us a guideline of how we, as believers, should pray in Mark 11. *"And whenever you stand praying, if you have anything against anyone, forgive him that your Father in heaven may also forgive you your trespasses. But if you do not forgive, neither will your Father in heaven forgive your trespasses."* (vs.25-26).

We learn through this example of prayer that we must be careful to forgive others first. Jesus is telling us that failure to forgive others will seriously inhibit God's response to our prayers.

— Un-forgiveness Hinders Christian Growth —

In Matthew 18:23-35, Jesus uses a parable to give us an illustration of forgiveness. He explains how the king had great compassion on his servant who was unable to pay the great debt that he owed. The king forgave him the debt, but when the king heard that this same servant refused to offer the same compassion and forgiveness to someone that owed him *a small debt*, he was grieved with his servant and threw him into prison. Verse 35 of that passage says, *"So My heavenly Father also will do to you if each of you, from his heart, does not forgive his brother his trespasses"*(Matt. 18:35).

Jesus is telling us that when He has offered us such matchless grace in forgiving all of our sin, He expects us to turn and offer the same grace to others who have wronged us.

The more I read about forgiveness in God's Word, the more I knew that I could not do this alone. I needed the supernatural power and strength of God to face these hurts! The chains and shackles around my heart were **stronger than my will to break them**. I began reading everything I could get my hands on about forgiveness.

— Power to Release the Offense —

The beginning of healing really started for me one night when I lay on my bed and spoke out loud to my Father in heaven all of the hurtful memories of a lifetime. From that time on, **forgiveness became a process more than any one act of the will**. We can never go back and change the past, but we can lay those memories on the cross with Jesus. It is a **choice** that we must make. Then, I read the wonderful promise in Philippians 2:13, *". . .for it is God who works in you both to will and to do for His good pleasure."*

This promise says to me that even when I struggle against my stubborn will to do what God wants me to do, I can point to this verse and ask God to give me the *desire* to obey him. I have learned that it is important to be honest with God about what is in my heart. **It helps me to see the truth in my heart that I may have been covering up. . .even from myself.** I have found that this is an important step in allowing Him to speak to us with His direction and purpose for our lives.

So many times I would put my finger on this verse and pray, "Lord, I don't want to obey you by loving this person," or "Lord, I don't want to forgive this person again, but I give you permission *to change my will to obey."*

This verse promises that He will do that for me. And if He has done it for me, He will do it for anyone who gives Him **permission to change his or her heart!**

Another wonderful verse in Paul's letter to the Philippians says, *". .being confident of this very thing, that He who has begun a good work in you will complete it until the day of Jesus Christ;"* (Phil. 1:6).

What a great promise! This promise says to me that God opened this can of worms, and He will complete His clean up and remodeling job in my heart, if it takes Him until He comes back again! But, what I discovered about myself was that I really did not want God to clean up that dark and secret room in my heart. I saved it away so that I could visit it from time to time and have my secret pity-party and feel sorry for myself! We sometimes hang on to our hurts and pains in order to take them out from time to time to satisfy some sense of justice. The choice to give God permission to enter this secret place is always a blow to the rule of *self* in our heart. We might even deceive ourselves here and pretend that we have forgiven everyone and everything. Until God helps us to see the contents of this ugly room in the cellar, we will do anything to keep from digging out the past. Then, when our feelings are hurt again, we often slip into that dark room and "snuggle up with the old smelly stench of *justifiable blame."*

I wanted to see changes in my heart instantly, but God began His work gradually in my heart. I had started using Mrs. Chas. E.

Cowman's little book, <u>Streams in the Desert</u>[8], for my morning devotional book. Through this little book, God began slowly, but surely, to influence my heart with His healing that flowed through the great heart of God to forgive such an undeserving people at such a great cost. The more I read of such total surrender to the sovereign love and grace of God through the words of this great woman of God, the freer I became to see with the eyes of Jesus. God used her book in so many ways to show me His sovereign, loving and forgiving heart. She showed me through her writings, the heart of the Cross; tenderly but firmly, morning by morning, until I began to see clearly that Jesus' love on that cross was more powerful than any hurt man could invoke on me or anyone else. Gradually, through God's grace, I was able to lay down the hurts and demands of my broken heart at the foot of the Cross. The more I looked at my Savior on that Cross, the less I needed to keep the memories of the past locked away in that secret place in my heart.

— **Power to Restore** —

There is real life changing power in forgiveness. It is so much more than an attitude or a word. It is a power that comes from God to heal and restore lives that have been shattered and broken by impossible circumstances. There began to grow in my heart such a love and forgiveness toward my mom that I could barely wait to see her again. I longed for the day when I could wrap my arms around her in love and tell her with all my heart how very much I loved and appreciated her. God's supernatural healing in my heart had opened this dark place that had been left closed and locked for most of my life. Sometimes when God does something this magnificent in a heart, we do not really understand it until we get past it and look back. All I really understood was that I had been set free. I felt like Jesus had stormed this ugly place in the cellar of my heart and thrown the doors wide open. He cleaned out all of the resentment and smelly demands for restitution that I was powerless to touch. All He was waiting for was my permission to enter this place. **Jesus will never invade the dark corners of our lives without our permission. Indeed, our invitation!** And to

---

[8] Streams In The Desert, by Mrs. Chas. E. Cowman. © 1950 by Cowman Publications, Inc. All Rights Reserved.

be completely honest, He even changed my will to want Him to (Phil. 2:13). So you see, without Him and His power to work in my heart, I still would be bound in this ugly warped state of un-forgiveness!

I have met and taught, and longed to help so many Christians, who try to carry on in the misconception that, "Now that I am a Christian, there is nothing else to worry about! These feelings and resentments are just something that I now have to cover-up, and if I become 'good enough' they will all go away!"

Others can see the fears and resentments in us, but are usually rebuffed with an attitude of denial if they dare to approach us with questions and suggestions. "After all, I am a Christian!"

I really thought that this was the end of this problem of forgiveness for me, but I was to learn that there were other secret places locked away that I had not yet allowed God to enter.

A few years ago, we decided that we should make a greater effort to visit my dad and stepmother in the south. My dad was now in his mid-eighties, and although very healthy and active, I knew that this could change quickly. I had felt all of my life a sense of disinterest from my father toward me. I often agonized over a possible reason for his lack of caring, but over a lifetime I had sadly learned to leave it as one of my life's "unsolved mysteries." Perhaps he felt that my mother had infected me with her bitterness toward him, or maybe he thought that I was too much like her and would judge him for the past. As we began to visit on a yearly basis, I discovered that I was more like him than my mother, in many ways. I have learned from raising three daughters of my own that we usually seem to have the most conflict with the one who is the most like us in personality. Someone has said, "We don't like our faults when we see them in our children."

This rejection or avoidance of me did not just begin with these visits. It had always been true, except for the warm memories of a special relationship with him before my parents were divorced. Friends have suggested to me that this aloofness was possibly his reaction to feelings of guilt for his abandonment.

— Binding and Loosing —

My heart longed for the opportunity to talk with him about the past. I wanted, and prayed for, an opportunity to reestablish a father-daughter relationship with him. During the last ten years of my dad's life, I made it a regular practice to visit their home in Mississippi for a short visit over his birthday. We sometimes attended church with them and tried to do things that pleased them both. Maybe his rejection of me was just an old fashioned "man thing." He often spoke of a man's sons as if they were sacred, or at least, an important reason to boast. I always doubted that anyone could really use this as a reason not to care about his, or her, daughter. The conclusion, I really felt, deep inside, was the same conclusion that haunted me all of my life: "there must be something unacceptable about me!" I could not remember in all of the years growing up, ever having received a birthday card from him, or heard him say a tender word of recognition that he thought or cared about me at all.

With each of the many visits during those years, I secretly hoped that this time I might measure up. However, each departure left me empty and sure that this would never happen. What was I struggling to accomplish, and why did it matter so much? My dad seemed to bristle toward me with only the slightest provocation.

Just before our planned trip to see them in the fall of 1999, my stepmother fell and broke her hip, revealing bone cancer in her leg. She was hospitalized and undergoing chemotherapy at the time of our arrival. My dad, now 91, was obviously overwhelmed and disoriented by all of these events. His world was crumbling about him, and his wife of over 50 years could no longer care for him the way she always had. When I talked with him on the phone, prior to our trip, he had encouraged me to come quickly, so that I could take care of him. However, my dad was so demanding and critical of my every move, any thoughts of pleasing him were soon abandoned as hopeless. He quickly transferred all of his frustration onto me. His responses toward me were short and his words curt and impatient. His criticism and disapproval, coupled with the 90° late September heat, became almost unbearable.

I prayed for patience and constantly reminded myself of God's command in the Bible to, honor my father and my mother (Exod. 20:12).

My stepmother, who was 19 years younger than my dad, recovered from the hip replacement and even the serious encounter with bone cancer in her leg and returned home from the hospital. During the following year my dad became hallucinatory and very abusive to her. He often saw imaginary people in the house and thought my stepmother was someone else. His reactions became violently dangerous and soon resulted in his commitment to the psychiatric ward at the hospital. In October of 2000, my stepmother called me with the news that he was in a coma and might not live many more days.

I bowed my head on the kitchen table and sobbed with an agony so great that it seemed to well up from the very core of my being.

I spoke out loud to God, "No, Lord, please don't let him die and leave me with this great burden in my heart!"

I was torn between this deep need within my own heart and an intense anger toward him that he would dare to die before he set things right between us. I had bowed before the Lord so many times with a sincere heart to forgive my father for the emptiness and pain he had caused in my life. Why couldn't I be free of this anger toward him? I had forgiven my mom completely and the beauty of our relationship that followed had been a wonderful gift from the Lord. Why was my heart so **bound** with this need? Need for what? I could not even understand this bondage that seemed to stifle me when I was around him. Why did I need so desperately for him to ask for my forgiveness, or to just say he was sorry, just once? That sounds like such a simple thing, but the bondage that I held in my heart was far more serious than that. I had not needed for my mother to ask forgiveness. Why did this seem to be so stuck in my spirit? I knew now, that he would probably die and I would be left with this unfinished ache deep within my soul.

As I sobbed, I seemed to be aware of the presence of the Lord next to me. He seemed almost visible to my spirit and began to counsel me.

"You must forgive him unconditionally." were His words to my spirit.

I raised my head almost expecting to see Him standing next to me.

"But Lord, I **have**, so many times!" was my audible response.

His next words pierced my heart with truth. "You have conditions," He said.

When the Lord speaks so clearly to your spirit, the words do not even pause at your mind. His spirit speaks volumes to your spirit faster than you can even comprehend. The revelation of His truth draws back a curtain in your whole being, so that you cannot miss His meaning. It was to me, as if a huge dam broke in my heart and I saw clearly what I had hidden from myself in my righteous cover-up.

"Yes!" I sobbed. "I waited all these years for him to say he was sorry!"

Why couldn't he acknowledge me with the love that I needed? That was all that I wanted, but I knew now that he never would. If he had lived another 100 years, I don't think there is anything I could ever do or be that would change that. As the Lord's truth pierced my broken heart, I felt His love surround me with an urgency to face this great issue now before my dad's death. In that moment, His love met me with the strength to completely lay it all down, for the first time in my life. I spoke the words of complete healing forgiveness out loud to the Lord.

"Yes, Lord, I forgive my dad, unconditionally." The truth of the moment swept through my heart giving me the ***power to choose to forgive*** in the same way Jesus forgave me.

I now accepted the fact that I could never do it on my own. I must have, and receive, His supernatural power of forgiveness within me to accomplish my release! In an eternal moment, I agreed with my Lord that I needed His power to unconditionally forgive my dad. In that moment my heart was set free! The healing rolled over my being with such joy that I felt new all over. I had carried this terrible burden all of my Christian life, but I knew now that **I had chosen to carry it.** God had approached me with tenderness and love, as well as the clarity and urgency that I needed at that moment. Now, my sobs were sobs of freedom. *What a mystery!*

I have often thought of the incredible visit with my Savior at that moment, as my dad lay in a coma in a Mississippi hospital only a few hours before his death. Was that amazing encounter with God for me? Or was it for him? Was my dad within moments of stepping into eternity? I don't understand it all, but I do know that the conversation that I had with my Savior in that moment, set my heart free. The call came within a few hours that my dad had awakened from the coma and then quietly passed into eternity with God.

My demand for restitution had become bondage in my own heart, and perhaps in some way had bound his heart, as well. The pain within me had locked onto my demands so stubbornly that I could not let go. This is a great mystery and is very hard to understand, but I know that it was true in my life. *Un-forgiveness toward another not only binds us with unseen chains and shackles, but it also binds those in our lives that it targets.* This is one of those truths that we have difficulty getting around with our mind of logic and reason. We do not think that way. These mysteries are unreasonable to the natural mind.

We must remember that the Bible says that the Christian must live by faith (Heb. 10:38). Our whole walk with God must be governed by faith instead of reason!

This is an issue that each Christian must resolve if they desire to walk in the fullness of Christian victory. As I have chosen to accept the things that are beyond my understanding. . .by faith, they have become so reasonable to my very being that I no longer see them an unreasonable! I believe that this is another mystery of the Christian's gift of spiritual eyesight.

We still struggle with this issue of the human spirit called, "my rights!" I have the "right" to withhold forgiveness as, a sort of, substitute revenge.

"I will just keep this as my secret punishment of him! I certainly do not owe him anything!"

But the mysteries of God are deeper than that. Jesus said to His disciples, "*. . .whatever you bind on earth will be bound in heaven, and whatever you loose on earth will be loosed in heaven*" (Matt. 18:18).

I feel that the visit that I had from my Savior just before my father passed into eternity was because of the mysterious truth of these words. **I do not believe that my refusal to forgive in any way would have. . .could have. . .kept my dad from his appointment with heaven**, but I do believe that God placed an urgency on my release of him just before his death perhaps because of the serious bondage in my own heart. Don't ask me to explain it. I cannot! But, I believe that it is eternally true because of the legal binding that God has put on the work of the cross! God the Father accepts the blood of His Son as legal payment for my sin and your sin when we receive Jesus as our Savior. There is a transaction that takes place before the throne of God, and we pass from death to life. When we refuse to forgive another who sins against us, Jesus says that God will not forgive our sins." (Mark 11:26)

We cannot take half of an agreement! When God prepared His gift to us, He placed redemption and forgiveness together in the same package (Matt. 6:14-15)! *This is another one of the great mysteries of God!*

The freedom of forgiveness was not in the words I said, for I had said them many times before and had truly meant them. The healing came with my response to the complete truth that the Lord revealed to me concerning my own heart! I had lacked the power within myself to

106

release my will. I surely knew better, for my Savior had walked this same bridge with me many years ago in forgiving my mother. I had often counseled and taught other women with these powerful truths. What emotional locks within our own soul hinder us from heeding our own counsel? Why had forgiveness toward my dad been so difficult to release into the loving, nail scared hands that hung on that cross for me? Perhaps the pain of a lifetime caused me to blame my dad more. Why had it been so important to have him confess his wrong? My dad's stubborn pride had refused to even acknowledge any responsibility for my hurt. I do not really know the reasons, but I know that the moment I lay my demand for restitution at the foot of the cross, my dad was set free. And I was free. I know that our Savior cares deeply and tenderly for His children's pain and will be faithful to meet us when we surrender our stubborn struggle to solve our need "our way."

When I went to my father's funeral and stood at his coffin, the miraculous freedom in my heart was almost beyond reality for me. I stood there thinking of how painful it would have been if God had not set me free just a few days before. I wept tears of sadness that we could not share a special time together and wondered what it would have been like. I know that we have much to share someday when we meet together with Jesus.

An incident happened one night a few years ago that made me terribly aware of the serious consequences of spiritual bondage connected with un-forgiveness. I was getting ready for bed one evening and it seemed as if the Spirit of God said to me, "Pray for ____!" I was so struck by this direct message to my spirit that I stopped what I was doing and found a quiet place to pray for this person who happened to be the wife of a pastor from a church in our city. I had had the privilege of speaking for the women of her church and had come to love her dearly. God had taught me years earlier not to pray out of my own knowledge, but to ask God to show me how to pray. The impression on my heart was to ask God to work out His forgiveness in her heart toward her husband. I later called her to inquire about her need and she wept with the realization that she had refused to forgive him for something between them. She shared with me days later that she had gone to him with a heart of complete forgiveness toward him and he had wept with freedom from a bondage that had bound his entire ministry. The next Sunday, God's anointing was released over him and many, many people responded to the gospel of Jesus Christ.

People sometimes use God's warning about refusing to forgive in Matthew 6:14-15 as a club. In other words, "You are supposed to be a Christian. If you don't forgive me for what I have done to you, then God will not forgive you of your sins, either!"

This statement, or something similar, is designed to invoke a sense of guilt on the person that has been wronged. Then, the wronged person is expected to knuckle under and restore the person to the same status that they enjoyed before. Just like that, trust should be restored. Most people when they say something like this, either to themselves or to others, don't understand the heart of God's teaching about forgiveness, and/or they really do not know God at all.

Before I understood the heart of God's Word, both to me and about me, these verses were terrifying pressure to "just get over it!" I thought that as a Christian, I was supposed to say, "I forgive," and then somehow forget that it ever happened. There were times when this *was* possible, but forgiveness for the deep hurts was not that simple. I tried to make it that simple, but the power to respond in this way was just not in me! I had a **wounded spirit** and the pain was deeply imbedded throughout my whole being as a person. I was unable even after I forgave those who had betrayed me, to forget what they had done, but I was able to leave it at the foot of the cross and no longer be angry or resentful toward the offender. And, yes! I was able to love them with the love of Jesus Christ! When God worked in me to give me His power to forgive, it did set me free. Free to love them; free to be with them without the pain; and yes, the freedom to be touched by them again.

There is the passage in Isaiah 43 where God is speaking to Israel about their failure to honor Him, even though He has covered them with His blessing. He says in the 25th verse of this chapter that He blots out their transgressions and He will not remember them.

While I believe that these verses refer specifically to God's working in the nation of Israel for a specific time, I do believe that they still apply to us in that the Bible says that God is the same yesterday, today and forever (Heb. 13:8). Another promise of His amazing forgiveness is recorded for us in the book of Psalms: *"As far as the east is from the west, so far has He removed our transgressions from us"* (Psalm 103:12).

I believe that God's forgiveness promises in these verses and in Isaiah 43:25 that He will not remember our sin **against** us. The debt has now been placed on Jesus and He no longer requires payment from you and me for the sin. However, the consequence of the sin almost always leaves altered circumstances in its wake. Through His forgiveness, He releases us from the penalty of the sin and our relationship with Him remains intact.

We read many accounts where mighty servants of God have been forgiven, but still must bear serious consequences for their action. Even though God forgave David for his adultery and murder, he and Bathsheba were denied the life of their son. Even though God forgave Moses for his anger in striking the rock, he was denied the right to take the Israelites into the Promised Land. Hebrews 12:10-11 tells us that God disciplines us for our good. Perhaps this is where we, as parents, learned to say to our children that their punishment was for their own good?

There are times when a relationship has been seriously injured or broken by one of the participants and **restitution** is needed to restore trust and to promote proper and just healing. Then there may also be times when one who has been seriously injured by another person's action may need time to heal, as well as a planned program to rebuild trust. This does not mean that the offended one is refusing to forgive. We have adopted the misconception that in the Christian realm, forgiveness is a word that magically makes it happen. Forgiveness, as we have already discussed, is so much more than, "I'm sorry". God's power of forgiveness in our hearts is restoration. . .and joy, and freedom!

Sometimes, an offense might be so severe that the relationship can never be restored to its former state, even though the offender has been forgiven. This is sometimes true when an offender has seriously violated a position of trust. People refer to God's forgiveness as our pattern, and it should be, but we need to discover the true heart of God's forgiveness and not our version. We do have the power "in Christ" to forgive completely, and continue to love with the power of the love of Jesus Christ in us, but I have never heard anyone testify to their ability to blot out the memory of the person's offense from their mind. The beauty is that just as God forgives and still loves us completely with His matchless love, so do we "in Christ" have that ability to forgive and yet love with Calvary Love. I do not believe that this forgiveness and love requires that we continue on as though nothing ever happened. When there is brokenness and true repentance of sin, the beauty of forgiveness in Christ often moves the relationship with another to a higher and more beautiful level of grace.

Quite a few years ago, I was teaching a group of women in a home Bible study. We had spent many weeks and months together and had grown to love and support each other in a special way. One morning one of the young women asked for special prayer for her sister's teenage daughter who had become pregnant with the child of her boyfriend. She asked that we pray for God's guidance for her sister who was very angry with her daughter and had a very drastic solution in mind. My heart was instantly broken for this young woman that I had never met. We learned that the mother of the teen had herself become pregnant out of marriage with her daughter who was now pregnant. The young woman in the class confirmed that the girl's mother had seemed to display anger and resentment toward the girl all of her life. Then, when I inquired, the young woman confirmed that her older sister had also been the product of a pregnancy outside of marriage, and had been forced by her parents to marry the young man. She, too, had always felt that her baby had ruined her life. Three generations of un-forgiveness had bound the hearts and lives of these women. This bondage could have gone on for many more generations if the blood of Jesus Christ and His forgiveness had not intervened. The young woman in the class went to her sister and shared what God had shown her about the power of forgiveness to release all three of the women in her family and restore their lives to be healthy free women. The mother of the teen saw for the first time in her life what the terrible sin of un-forgiveness had done in her life and in the life of her daughter. Her heart was broken. She not only forgave her daughter, but her mother as well. God's love and forgiveness healed and restored this whole family, and saved possibly three more generations from the same bondage.

After David's great sin with Bathsheba and the murder of Uriah, the prophet Nathan confronted David (2 Sam. 12:12-14), about his sin. David immediately repented of his sin, but Nathan goes on to tell David of the punishment that would be levied against him for his sin. God explains to David in 2 Samuel 12:12-14 why he must suffer severe consequences for his sin, even though God *"put away his sin"*.

110

— <u>70 X 7</u> —

There is also the question of repetitious sin; someone who keeps doing the same thing against you over and over, and over again. I have heard others, and myself, comment on the fact that they are sick and tired of having to forgive someone the same old sin over and over. This same feeling prompts us to ask God for an answer. In other words, at what point can I pull the plug on forgiveness?

"After all, forgiving them once was hard enough. They will never change, anyway."

Jesus' answer to each of us is Luke 17:4, *"And if he sins against you seven times in a day, and seven times in a day returns to you, saying, 'I repent,' you shall forgive him."* Verse 4 of this passage is often one of the most difficult for us. Jesus says that even if a person keeps committing the same offense over and over in the same day and he still repents, you must forgive that person again and again. I can almost hear myself saying to that person,

"I'm sick and tired of having to forgive you over and over again."

We learn in this passage in Luke that we not only need God's love to forgive, but we also need God's patience to keep on forgiving! We have all experienced the incredible freedom and deliverance that "God patience" has afforded us and we have surely wept at God's matchless grace that keeps on forgiving us over and over again!

One of the most important things to know and remember about the amazing forgiveness by God toward man is that it requires repentance for sin (1 John 1:9). Man must admit his sin before God and repent, or turn from, his sin before he can receive the gift of forgiveness. Jesus paid the redemptive price for our sin, at the great cost of His death on Calvary. When one of us bows before Him and asks forgiveness for our sin, God the Father transfers our sin onto His Son, Jesus, and marks the debt of our sin canceled. God's example of forgiveness toward us is our example toward others. We must use wisdom and love toward one who needs to come to the place of repentance and restoration.

— **Power to Forgive Myself** —

There have been other struggles in my life to forgive, but none greater than the almost impossible struggle to **forgive myself**. This one was the hardest of all, perhaps, because I blamed myself for my hurt more than I blamed anyone else.

This is a dangerous pitfall for anyone who has experienced the heartbreaking rejection by those who are expected to stand between the Billy Goat Gruffs of life and a child's vulnerable heart for protection. Because of the great need for someone to love you, especially a mother or father, the child prefers to blame himself. A child of rejection will hold onto any thread of hope, no matter how thin. To openly blame those that you desperately need could possibly risk the loss of their favor, so you **blame yourself**.

"There must be something wrong with me to make them throw me away."

The sum total of the child's thought is usually, "It must be my fault."

The child's heart sees many other children, who are not perfect, but are loved and protected by their parents. The only possible answer is that, "I must be a really awful person!"

There are so many children that endure painful criticism and anger at the hands of adults in their lives who begin to experience the same acceptance of blame. This becomes a terrible burden on the heart of a child and eventually will produce a *wounded spirit*. This wounded spirit handicaps the child emotionally and if not corrected, may last a lifetime.

Guilt and **blame** are two of the most lethal weapons that the destroyer uses against the Christian. For one who has suffered with a wounded spirit, the habit of carrying this guilt and blame is a very serious and dangerous weakness in his armor. The enemy knows this and because he watches our lives, he knows the soft spots in our defenses. He uses these lies against us that he has gotten away with a hundred times, and because they still cause us to buckle, he continues to succeed over and over again.

Jesus tells us that John 10:10 *"The thief does not come except to steal, and to kill, and to destroy."* The truth is that he cannot succeed in heaping guilt and blame on us, unless we let him! This is one of the response habits that we must break.

I remember the day when the Holy Spirit showed me the depth of un-forgiveness that I had harbored and even nurtured in my own heart toward myself. One day during my prayer time with the Lord, I found myself asking forgiveness over and over again. Then, I began to ask myself, why? Why had I felt the need to keep on asking forgiveness when close examination of my heart had not revealed any known sin that I had overlooked?

As I asked God in prayer to show me what was going on inside, the Holy Spirit revealed to me that I held deep resentment toward myself for being unacceptable. God drew back another curtain in my heart, which revealed a label of "worthless" left there by many years of agreeing with the world. When God showed me that I must forgive myself, I still had to conquer the habit of self-accusation and blame that had been established over a lifetime. I had already learned that this business of forgiveness can only be accomplished through the indwelling power of Jesus Christ in my life, so I willingly laid the whole burden at the foot of the cross. I audibly spoke forgiveness to myself before God, and then received that forgiveness, "in the name of Jesus."

This was the beginning of freedom in my heart, but there was still much to do to break the habit of blame toward myself. First, I asked the Holy Spirit to remind me when I fell into this familiar habit of blame. We so often travel the path of habit without realizing it until we find ourselves way beyond the point of no return. These habits establish patterns of thought that must be consciously broken through prayer and obedience to God's direction in His Word!

The Holy Spirit is always faithful to remind us when we ask Him to, but it takes a conscious choice to obey God, even after we have been faithfully reminded. *When we **choose to obey,** the power of God within our heart will help us to carry out His will to redirect our thoughts according to His will.*

We seem to expect God to judge and condemn us in the same way that we feel condemned whether by others or by ourselves. However, God tells us in Romans that if we are a "child of God," there is no condemnation in God's eyes! The blood of Jesus has made us "as white as snow" (Isa. 1:18). The way we *feel* does not change the truth of what God says about us, but it does usually cause us to go on living a life of defeat. It is difficult for someone who has suffered a deeply wounded spirit to break this habit of self-condemnation, but it is possible through the restorative power and love of Jesus Christ! Romans 8:1-2 says, *"There is therefore now no condemnation to those who are in Christ Jesus, who do not walk according to the flesh, but according to the Spirit."*

If God does not condemn me at all, then neither can I. What a loving God! What a great freedom He has given to me and to you.

"Beloved Father, You have sown the seeds of forgiveness in our hearts through the death of Your Son, Jesus. When we allow those seeds to sprout, take root, and grow, their blooms produce a fragrance so rare that even the most hardened soul is captivated by their beauty, and is drawn to the cross."

6

"The Bridge of Mystery Over The Great Desert of the Impossible"

— The Bridge of Faith —

— Allegory —

Without warning the beautiful green foliage that surrounds the valley begins to fade and the lush green landscape gives way to rugged terrain.

As the path winds through the changing landscape, the way begins to grow difficult and the heart begins to doubt that there could be a bridge constructed in such a hopeless desert wilderness. Battering winds assault your vision as you strain to make out the way ahead. Suddenly your feet stumble over a stone marker that seems to rise out of the sand like a mysterious guardian left there to lead you to this strange and mysterious bridge.

As you approach the great stone, seemingly left here by another traveler, your heart is struck by the strange, yet familiar words carved deep into its core.

"NOW FAITH IS THE SUBSTANCE OF THINGS HOPED FOR, THE EVIDENCE OF THINGS NOT SEEN"[9]

What could these words mean? . . .And why have they been left in such a lonely and forbidding place? The worn old bridge appears before you now, almost hopelessly abandoned in the weather-beaten desert wasteland.

Your first look at this structure invokes a disappointing sense of doubt that this bridge could actually support your weight should you venture to step onto its old weathered surface. Surely, this cannot be the way to continue. However, a quick inspection of the horizon shows that there is no other way to proceed from here and you have already decided at the beginning of this journey that you can never go back.

But as you take your first step onto the old bridge a strange sensation of movement begins within the structure beneath your feet. . .Almost like a stretching motion that begins to sing and bend with the weight of your every step. Your hands reach for the old railing that now is changing with your touch. An overwhelming sense of awe fills your heart as you realize that the old bridge seems to be transporting you to a new and amazing dimension of awareness and victory. Instinctively, you turn to view again the ancient stone with its words of promise, only to catch a look at the now magnificent bridge that you are crossing.

---

[9] Hebrews 11:1

"The Bridge of Mystery Over The Great Desert of the Impossible"
— The Bridge of Faith —

The Christian life, from beginning to end, is based on faith. Faith is the hand that opens the door of God's grace that leads to salvation through the blood of Jesus Christ (Eph. 2:8, 9).

Faith is the life-blood that flows through the veins of the one who walks in victory. The man or woman, who looks down the road and sees his lost and broken family restored at the feet of Jesus, does so by faith. The Abraham's and the Joshua's; and the Sam Patterson's; and you and I, step out into the arena of the impossible when God invites us to look at the world through His eyes. Those eyes do not see with the world's reasoning and checks and balances. Those eyes see mountains moved; nations with hands uplifted in praise; children playing at the feet of Jesus; marriages restored, and hearts and minds set free from addictions and bondage through the death and resurrection of His Son. God provides the faith to believe His truth. It is a gift from God, not something that we achieve on our own. But, it does involve our choice to believe that truth. The world says, "Show me, and I will believe." God says, "Believe Me, and I will show you!" Then, God begins the long process of teaching us and training us to walk in faith. That process takes a lifetime. Because we live in an instant society, we expect immediate results in our lives, but God in His patient training process knows what it will take in each of our lives to transform us into the image of Jesus Christ.

I have heard so many Christians say that their faith is not strong enough or that they "just cannot believe." Everything I have learned in my walk with Jesus Christ proves that this is just not true.

The Bible says that God has given to each person *"a measure of faith"* (Rom. 12:3). This means that each person has been given enough faith to believe the truth about God. The Bible also tells us in Romans 2:15 that from creation, the truth about God was *"written in their hearts, their conscience also bearing witness,. ."* In other words, God created men and women with a natural hunger and thirst to see and believe in God. We also read that God is *". . .not willing that any*

117

should perish, but that all should come to repentance" (2 Peter 3:9). In other words, it is God's will that each and every person born on this earth hear and believe the gospel of Jesus Christ! If God has given to each person the faith to believe, and it is His will that each person should believe, then what is the problem?

The problem is that God, in His great design, has given to each of us a sovereign will. The choice is yours and mine. We have the right to **choose** to believe God, or to deny belief in Him and His truth. Each time we choose to **ignore** God's opportunity to hear and accept Him, we are, in fact, choosing to deny Him! A person can deny God's truth, by an act of the will, so many times that his or her heart becomes callous and hardened to the truth by the repeated **choice of unbelief**. Hebrews 3:12 warns, *"Beware, brethren, lest there be in any of you an evil heart of unbelief in departing from the living God;"*

This became very clear to me one morning as I was teaching a class of women in Boulder, Colorado. This was a large class and I had asked the women to reserve their questions until the last 20 minutes of each class. Each day, I would close the teaching and hands would go up throughout the room. There was one woman who always sat near the front of the class that seemed quite agitated by parts of the teaching. She would openly comment at various intervals, which became very disruptive to the rest of the class. She always raised her hand for the questions, but usually verbalized a great deal of frustration at the biblical answers that she received. She just "could not believe the Bible", but she could not resist being there, either. After about the third week, I asked her to remain after the class so that I could spend time with her on a personal basis.

When the room cleared, we sat down together in front row seats. Her brow was wrinkled and angry and her voice was challenging. She said that she just could not believe these things that I was teaching and continued with a myriad of typical social questions that defied the truth of a loving God. I stopped her with the reassurance that I would gladly talk to her about all of her concerns, but that first, we needed to pray and ask for God's wisdom and guidance as we talked. I asked her if she objected and she said "no." I bowed my head and began to pray out loud, seeking God's revelation to me concerning the real needs in this woman's heart. I confessed to God that I did not know within myself what she needed, nor did I have the wisdom to answer any of her questions, but that I knew that He knew her, and loved her deeply.

Then, in the middle of my prayer, the Holy Spirit seemed to speak clearly to my heart, "Ask her to confess the sin of unbelief."

I stopped short in my prayer because I felt that I had received from God the key to this woman's salvation. I took her hands in mine and, as simply as I could, I began to tell her what God had said to me. She looked baffled and confused and said that she did not understand. She continued with the assurance that she had tried over and over to believe, but that it just "did not make sense." I could have started there and talked myself blue explaining why it did not make sense to her, but I knew that it would not make any difference in her heart. The Bible says in 1 Corinthians 2:14, *"But the natural man does not receive the things of the Spirit of God, for they are foolishness to him; nor can he know them, because they are spiritually discerned."*

The natural man in this verse means the man (or woman) that has not yet been "born again" by receiving Jesus Christ as Savior. This verse says that this person cannot understand the things of God because only the indwelling Holy Spirit that comes to live in the heart of a person can give understanding of spiritual truth. Therefore, at this point, she could not figure out why the Bible could not be reasoned out. It was as **unreasonable** to her as it is to most of the world today!

I then asked her if she would be willing to bow her head and ask God's forgiveness for the sin of unbelief.

"I will try anything," was her somewhat bewildered reply.

She bowed her head, and with halting words, asked God to forgive her for the sin of unbelief. We raised our heads and I began to share the gospel of Jesus Christ—no explanations, no excuses, just the simple child-like gospel of Jesus Christ. Her eyes became wide like a little child as the truth of the ages sank deep within her spirit.

"I see it!" She said.

Tears began to flow down her cheeks as God revealed His love for her through the death and resurrection of His Son, Jesus Christ! I sat there in awe as I watched this miracle of life in her spirit. We talked for a long time. Her dry spirit was like a sponge and she could not hear enough! She said that she no longer needed explanation for the questions that had previously plagued her mind because the eyes of her heart were now opened to God's truth. Her heart had been hardened by the repeated sin of unbelief until she could no longer receive God's truth. When she obeyed God's direction and confessed to Him her sin of unbelief, the "veil" over her heart (2 Cor. 3:16) was "taken away." Her spiritual eyes were opened. *A mystery?* Yes! But, God's life in us is filled with great and wonderful mysteries that I think will take eternity to see and understand. The Bible says in Hebrews 3:19, *"So we see that they could not enter in because of unbelief."* The children of Israel, referred to in this passage, were denied access to the Promised Land because of their *choice* not to believe God. The lesson still stands for us today. God seeks to reveal to each of us the truth of Who He is, many times in a lifetime. He may use a parent, a pastor, a friend, a Sunday school teacher, or a complete stranger, but if we refuse to receive God's truth over and over, our heart will become hardened to God's truth through the sin of unbelief. If we choose to receive His truth, He gives revelation to our spirit that opens the door to salvation and life.

This is why it is so important for parents to teach their children, by word and example, the wonderful truths of God's kingdom while they are very small. I once heard someone ask a great leader of the Christian faith when we should start teaching our children about Jesus Christ. His instant answer was, "The moment they are born." We know that a baby can hear and recognize their parents voices while still in the womb, and I have heard parents tell their unborn baby how much Jesus loves them. God gives us instruction concerning the important and effective spiritual training of our children in the book of Deuteronomy.

> *"And these words which I command you today shall be in your heart. You shall teach them diligently to your children, and shall talk of them when you sit in your house, when you walk by the way, when you lie down, and when you rise up."* (Deut. 6:6-7).

Faith is easily established in the heart of a small child *if* the child sees that faith lived out in the hearts and lives of his parents. This instruction concerning our children was not to the pastor or the Sunday school teacher, but to parents! We have a great responsibility to establish the truth about God in the hearts of our children. If a child sees love and honor toward God lived out in the behavior of his parents he will mirror that love and honor, even before he understands it.

The most treasured memory that I have as a Christian parent was the experience of leading my own little girls to believe in and receive

Jesus Christ as Savior. Each night we would snuggle together on one of their beds and read stories from the Bible from one of their devotion books written especially for their ages. There are so many beautifully written and illustrated books for children designed to draw their hearts to a believing understanding of the plan of salvation through Jesus Christ. Their little hearts were always thrilled with the pictures and stories, and they found it easy to relate the examples to their own lives and young experiences. They learned early, to pray out loud from hearts that found it easy to accept God's truth and love for them. There was no greater joy for me than that of seeing and hearing my little girls pray for Jesus to come into their hearts so that they could be *"born again."* There is no music in the whole world sweeter than the honest, believing prayer of a child.

Of course, adults can still believe on Jesus Christ and be saved. But, I believe that it is so much easier to come to Jesus as a child because a little child's heart is tender toward the truths of God. By the time we reach adulthood the world's passions with its reasoning and desires have so cluttered the heart that it becomes more difficult to see clearly the wonderful truths about God. This is why we hear so many testimonies of those who have suffered great loss by the world's standards before they could see clearly their need for a Savior. Some do not respond even then.

— God's Written Word —

There are four basic ways that God uses to teach faith to our hearts. The first, and I believe the most powerful, is **God's written Word**, The Bible. The Bible says in Hebrews 4:12, *"For the word of God is living and powerful, and sharper than any two-edged sword, piercing even to the division of soul and spirit, and of joints and marrow, and is a discerner of the thoughts and intents of the heart."*

There is no greater explanation of the Word of God than this one found in the 4th chapter of the book of Hebrews. Something powerful happens to individuals, to nations and peoples when they read and meditate on God's Word. The reason, of course, is that the written Word is God's expression of Himself and His Son, Jesus Christ. There is power within its pages to touch the most hardened criminal with new life; to open the eyes of the blind; to bring nations to their knees;

and to impart hope and peace to the hopeless and lost on any shore. The truth within its pages is baffling to the most learned scholar until the Spirit of God opens his eyes to see and understand as a little child.

In an earlier chapter, I shared how the sweet little elderly lady came to the little girl's dormitory when I was 11 and encouraged me to memorize chapters from the book of John in order to win prizes. My first assignment was to memorize the first chapter of the Gospel of John from a small booklet that she gave me. I remember walking back and forth on the sidewalk in front of the dormitory saying the words out loud, over and over again until they were perfect. They were established so deep in my heart that I remember many nights lying awake in the lonely darkness of my room, with only these words to comfort me. I did not know their meaning then, I only knew that they were mine. A few years later when Jesus Christ came into my life and began to reveal His truth to my heart, I knew that He had given me these powerful words to be a covering to guard my heart until that special appointment with Him at the age of 15.

> *"In the beginning was the Word, and the Word was with God, and the Word was God. He was in the beginning with God. All things were made through Him, and without Him nothing was made that was made. In Him was life, and the life was the light of men. And the light shines in the darkness, and the darkness did not comprehend it"* (John 1:1-5).

These verses are still a powerful anchor for my life, and I find myself still saying them out loud when I awake in the darkness. The New Living Translation says verse 5 like this, *"The light shines through the darkness, and the darkness can never extinguish it"* (John 1:5, NLT)

Many years ago I began keeping a journal which I used to write my deepest thoughts and prayers to God about His working in my life. There were times when I wrote almost daily, particularly when I was going through some of my most difficult trials. There were also many accounts of miracles and great praise for His amazing love toward me. Whatever the circumstance, those pages are still filled with yellowed clippings attached to many of the pages from daily devotions and Bible readings. Faith was built in my heart as I saw that the God of the universe was so deeply involved in my life. I was amazed then, and still am, that God inspires one of His servants to write a small devotion, perhaps months or even years ahead, that is specifically meant to touch my heart, or yours, on a particular day! Is this a coincidence? No! There are no coincidences in a Christian's life! The Bible tells us that, *"The steps of a good man are ordered by the Lord, And He delights in his way"* (Psa. 37:23).

Sometimes, when I have moments of sadness or discouragement I open the yellowed pages of that journal and weep with remembrance at God's amazing love and faithfulness toward me in every part of my life. When we read and study the Bible daily, it begins to settle deep within our spirit and establishes faith that will anchor our hearts against the fiercest storms. The Bible says, "So then faith comes by hearing, and hearing by the word of God" (Rom. 10:17).

— <u>Godly Instruction</u> —

The next way that God uses to teach faith to His children is <u>Godly Instruction</u>. Jesus commanded the disciples, and you and me, to go to all of the nations and teach them everything that He taught when He was here on earth (Matthew 28:19-20). This was part of His instruction before He returned to His Father after completing His assignment here on earth. We have a responsibility to teach others how to live and love according to God's commands in His Word. As we teach others how to carefully discern the right interpretation of God's Word (2 Tim. 2:15), we must be careful that our conduct also teaches the same true message!

> *"How then shall they call on Him in whom they have not believed? And how shall they believe in Him of whom they have not heard? And how shall they hear without a preacher?"* (Rom. 10:14-15).

God used instruction to whet the appetite of the young woman in the Bible class to question the truth and validity of the Bible that led to her acceptance and belief in Jesus Christ as her personal Savior.

— **Christian Example** —

The next vital way God uses to teach us faith is **Christian Example**. The old saying "one picture is worth a thousand words," is really true for each of us. When I was teaching Junior High School so many years ago, I would jokingly say to my students, "Don't do as I do, do as I **say** do!" Such a statement is surely foolishness. As we watch those in leadership around us, we, either consciously or unconsciously, begin to mirror the things that we admire in their lives. At important intervals in my life God brought alongside me, godly men and women of outstanding Christian character and beauty to teach me by example, how to walk in faith. These special people mirrored Jesus' life in every part of their daily walk. As I watched their exemplary lives of peace, strength and beauty, I wanted to be like them. These great men and women of God made it seem like such an easy thing for me to believe what God said to me in His Word. These giants of faith and integrity influenced me deeply. I watched each of these beautiful men and women demonstrate great faith and trust in the God of the impossible. I believe that these immovable giants of Christianity were brought alongside my life at God's perfect and precise timing to fashion and mold the bridge of faith that God wished to build and strengthen in my life. Their impact on my life created in me the desire to turn and build bridges for others who would come after me.

The Bible says that we are *"Ambassadors for Christ"* (2 Cor. 5:20). We are representing Him and His kingdom to the world. Someone has said that your life might be the only Bible that some people ever read. This is a big responsibility, and one that we must be careful to guard. There are so many that will be watching our lives just the way we have watched the exemplary lives of others. Our children; the neighbors; the store clerk; the hairdresser; the person in line that abuses us; they are all hoping to see a real Christian; perhaps someone they can talk to about their hurt or their questions about God. God uses our example to teach faith to others! We should constantly ask ourselves if God can trust us to make others hungry and thirsty to know Jesus in a personal way, or does our behavior actually reinforce a negative opinion of Christianity from others?

— **Demonstration** —

The fourth basic way that God uses to teach faith to His children is **Demonstration**. The Bible tells us that the cross of Jesus Christ is God's ultimate demonstration of His love toward man. *"But God demonstrates His own love toward us, in that while we were still sinners, Christ died for us"* (Rom. 5:8). The cross of Jesus Christ; His death and resurrection—is God's great demonstration of His magnificent love for man. Jesus Christ, God in the flesh: the Creator of the world; stepped from eternity into our world with the purpose of taking in His own body the sins of mankind, so that by faith we might pass from the penalty of death into life with God for all eternity. Wow!

Demonstration is the cement; the practical application designed by God to show us that we really can trust Him to do what He says He will do. We really do not seem to pay close attention to God's miraculous provision for all of our needs until we need something that we cannot supply ourselves!

Our way is to say, "Yes, Lord, I trust you to protect me through deep waters! I am absolutely sure of it!" But, until we find ourselves in deep waters without a lifeboat, we do not know for sure that He really will supply the life jacket! We say that we trust Him to supply all of our needs (Phil. 4:19), but until we **really** need Him to meet a need that we cannot supply ourselves, we will not seek His provision. He will prepare a well planned, tailor-made demonstration that will teach us of His great love and provision. This is the cement that establishes the lessons from His Word solidly in our hearts. Rarely does one learn how to completely trust God to do miraculously according to all He says He will, until He gives us an attention getting demonstration.

One of the greatest demonstrations in my own life happened while I was living in Kansas City. I had been asked to be Chairman of the Johnson County Christian Women's Club. This was, and is, a lovely organization for women established to share the gospel of Jesus Christ to women through lovely monthly luncheons. However, there were many neighborhoods in our area that we felt were not yet being reached by the monthly luncheons. One of the Advisors and I had discussed this often and decided to begin meeting for prayer, seeking a plan from God that would reach out to every woman in Johnson County in a unique and beautiful way. As we prayed, God gave us a plan. We would have a garden tea at one of the beautiful mansions in Mission

Hills. Mission Hills was one of the most affluent neighborhoods in Johnson County Kansas. This mansion must be so well known that every woman in Johnson County would want to attend. We sat down with the women at Stonecroft Ministries and shared with them the vision that God had given us. They gave us their blessing and agreed to pray for God's guidance as we proceeded with the plans. As we met and prayed together over a period of time, we began to ask God to formulate every part of the plan, including the date and the time of day. We started with a list of three mansions, found their phone numbers in the phone book and began our quest with fear and trembling. The first one on our list did not answer the phone. The next one was the Russell Stover mansion of Russell Stover Candies.

We prayed and asked God to have Mrs. Stover answer the phone instead of one of her servants. She answered the phone on the first try! I was so shocked and nervous that the jumbled words tumbled out of my mouth in such profusion that I was even confused by my explanation to her for the call.

When I came up for air, her answer was, "Yes!" I was so shocked I think I again repeated my reason for calling.

She said again, "Yes, you may have your tea in my garden."

I asked her if we might come out to her home to meet her and discuss our plans with her. She again said, "Yes."

She set a time for us to come and as soon as I hung up the phone, we squealed like children at this impossible favor from God. We were so light-headed we almost fainted. We then dropped to our knees and thanked our miraculous God for the door that He had opened before us. We knew that God would do a magnificent thing with this Garden Tea. We also knew that we must be careful not to get ahead of Him, but to wait on Him for every answer as we proceeded with His plan to touch all of Johnson County with the glory and power of His gospel!

When the day arrived for our meeting with Mrs. Stover, we were concerned about making a good impression on this grand lady. We giggled as we agreed to take my friend's beautiful Cadillac for the trip. As we pulled onto the grounds of the magnificent old mansion, we were already in awe that this was happening. One of the servants met us at the door and showed us into a drawing room off the massive foyer. We were seated when Mrs. Stover entered the room and the pleasant lady who greeted us was not at all what we had expected. She could have been a neighbor down the street. She was friendly and very down-to-earth, but very businesslike as she listened to the information that we presented to her about Christian Women's Clubs and our vision to use her beautiful garden to attract many women to hear the gospel of Jesus Christ. She seemed to like the idea and said that she would have her swimming pool painted and her garden prepared for the occasion. She asked if she could invite her two sisters from Chicago and California to attend.

Then she began to list her **conditions** for the event. She said that she had had other events in her home and that people had been so rude as to remove the bathroom towel bars from the wall as souvenirs. Because of this and other circumstances, she made it very clear that no one would be allowed inside her home, not even to use the bathroom, and not even in case of rain. We did not even blink at this because these were God's plans and not ours! She said that the food must be catered and kept in trucks at a designated place outside the home. We agreed to all of her conditions. Then we asked *her* to set the date and the time for the tea. She pulled out a calendar and gave us the date of **May 20, between 2 and 4 p.m**.

The next 4 to 6 weeks were filled with planning, praying and arrangements. The large committee sent out invitations, using the phone book from all over the county. One of the most exclusive shops in Kansas City was invited to present a spring fashion show around her freshly painted pool. A caterer was hired and hundreds of chairs were rented for seating. Mrs. Stover had truckloads of beautiful flowers brought in and planted in beds all over the expansive grounds. We were always very careful to remind ourselves that this was God's vision, and not ours!

When the morning for the tea arrived, I was awakened to gray and heavy skies overhead. I ran to the television to listen to the weather forecast for the afternoon. The weatherman showed the threat of tornadoes throughout the whole area. I was stunned! This was the one possibility that we had overlooked. May usually meant violent weather in Kansas City and often terrifying tornadoes plagued the city. There were horns mounted on poles throughout the whole metro area that would blow loud, repeated warnings to "take cover" as the storms threatened the city. Many times during past years, I had grabbed my little girls and rushed to the basement during the month of May to wait under a large table until the horns stopped blowing those frightening blasts of danger. How could we have planned this for May? My heart almost stopped as I thought of all the plans and money we had invested. Christian Women's Club does not have a budget for such things. Our budget was faith; faith that many, many women would attend and the bills would be paid out of the attendance fees. Had we missed God? Even as the question formed in my heart, I knew that we had not! I whispered a prayer that He would help me keep my heart and eyes focused on Him, and not on circumstances!

My phone began to ring. The advisor, who was now my precious friend and confidante, called and asked me if I had seen the weather report. I think I was in shock. How could this be happening? My friend and I agreed that we would wait and trust, for we had come too far to begin second-guessing God's leading now. We once again examined our hearts and agreed that we would remain strong and immovable before the rest of the committee.

The sky grew darker and darker as I donned the new spring dress and wide-brimmed hat I had splurged to buy for the occasion. The committee had agreed to arrive at Mrs. Stover's home around 11 am to set up chairs in preparation for the hundreds of reservations that we had received. The committee was huddled under umbrellas as a light drizzle of rain began to fall from the heavily overcast skies. Committee chairmen watched my face in puzzlement as I heard myself assure them that God would surely complete what He had begun. We would trust Him to finish the vision! These were not our plans, and we had not entered into any part of them on our own.

Around noon the skies overhead were so black that cars were driving with their headlights on like it was nighttime. Chills ran through our hearts as the horns began to blow with warnings of tornadoes in the area. Committee members began to approach me with anxious urging to call the whole thing off. I could not! You must believe me, this was not stubbornness or arrogance or any kind of defense of my own plans. Our faith was being severely tested and if, for some reason God rained us out, then we would still trust Him! Somehow I knew that God would do all that He said He would! There are those times in our Christian walk that God calls on us to walk completely alone with Him. This was one of those terrifying times!

The boutique reminded us that we would be liable if one drop of rain ruined one of their beautiful creations. The caterers sat in their trucks that were filled with trays and boxes of cakes and finger sandwiches especially designed for the occasion. Women moved through the rows of seats wiping wet chairs that were once again filled with raindrops as fast as they wiped them dry.

I struggled to keep my heart focused and silently looked for someone to help me bear this heavy burden. Questions bombarded my thoughts; questions of money and "what ifs!" I asked Mrs. Stover if I could call the committee into her foyer for prayer.

Her reply to me was, "Honey, I wouldn't miss this for anything in the world!"

We joined hands in a circle, including Mrs. Stover and her two sisters, and asked God to examine our hearts. **We prayed for God's glory alone**. We asked if we had in some way disobeyed Him or done this for the wrong reasons, to please send us a downpour, otherwise, we would trust Him that the tea would take place at 2 p.m. We submitted our hearts and our will to His, whatever it was. We prayed that He would fill our hearts with courage to obey Him and to trust Him regardless of the dark and stormy skies.

As we walked out of the foyer into the blackness, the rain began to slow to a light drizzle again. All of the women went about their assignments with new resolve. Around 1:30, the rain stopped and the caterers and the florist began to unload their trucks at the committee members bidding. Even though the skies were still dark and overcast, women began to arrive for the tea. The numbers were drastically diminished, but we were amazed that *anyone* came. Myrtle Baron, the National Director of Christian Women's Clubs, who was the speaker for the day. arrived and her face was radiant with Jesus, as always. I breathed a prayer of joy for her lovely presence. Women began to take their places at the tables that had been prepared with fresh flowers for the occasion as we continued to wipe the hundreds of chairs.

As I took my place at the head table, along with Myrtle Baron, the soloist, and Mrs. Stover, I remember the women's faces that were there. Their expressions seemed to be expressions of curiosity more than anything else. Had they come just to see what would happen when the bottom dropped out? I dismissed that thought in the name of Jesus, and once again prayed for faith.

At 2 p.m., I stood up to welcome the women to the Garden Tea and **at that precise moment God rolled back the clouds like a scroll!** Every mouth dropped and each woman audibly gasped at the brilliant sunshine that instantly flooded the grounds! Every face turned toward the sky that was now bathed in sunshine. We could barely choke back the tears of joy at this incredible miracle that we were witnessing. I stood speechless with my face turned toward the heavens and the beautiful blue sky above us. For the next two hours, God's miracle of brilliance warmed the garden with beauty, but none more beautiful than the breathless praise of hearts left speechless by His hand. Mrs. Stover and her sisters sat with their mouths open in stunned silence and Mrs. Stover told us later that she would never forget what God had done in her garden that afternoon.

When Myrtle Baron stood to speak, she opened with the words; "Our God is not dead!" She spoke of God's truth and faithfulness and His gift of love to each woman there. But the most powerful message to each of us that afternoon was that we were in the presence of the God that spoke the world into being with the Word of His mouth! We were humbled by His power and majesty; and yes, His love that would move before our eyes to **glorify Himself** in our presence. We did not have the numbers we had wanted, but there were exactly enough women to pay every bill we had incurred. God had chosen to work out His plan just as we had asked; that **He alone would be glorified**! Had our plans worked out with hundreds and hundreds of women, without the stormy skies, would we have seen His hand in such a magnificent way? Would this tea have been any different from any other tea prepared in a garden full of women? Would we have learned that we could trust Him to keep His Word in the middle of the storm? I still marvel at the incredible circumstances surrounding God's plan. I learned a lesson that day about my great and mighty God. I learned that **God's precision always defines His hand!**

At exactly 4 p.m., the black clouds closed over Johnson County like a window shade dropping over the sun! Within minutes, the horns were once again blowing their warnings to "take cover!" But, we had been a part of a miracle of God that day! Nothing could frighten our hearts now! We knew that God had attended this tea that He had planned, and He had surely been glorified! Someone on the committee called the next day and told us that there had been a small article in the newspaper that morning that commented on the strange events in the weather the day before. We knew, and Mrs. Stover and her sisters knew, each of the women at the tea knew, and even the women that had canceled knew that God's power was real and His Word was true! We could not have asked for more than this! What a magnificent demonstration we had witnessed from His hand! **None of us would ever be the same again!**

Myrtle Baron wrote a beautiful poem about the miraculous events of that day which she gave to me as a gift a few weeks later. I have it framed and hanging on the wall next to my computer. Each time I look up and see it hanging there, I am once again astounded to have witnessed such a magnificent demonstration of His love and power.

I will always be baffled at the way God poured His faith into my heart for this task. I discovered then that **God always supplies the faith to accomplish the task that He asks us to perform.** As I have read and studied accounts of ordinary people in His Word that performed great acts of faith and obedience, I know that they, too, must have been stunned that God used them in such a way.

There have been so many demonstrations of God's provision in my life that it would take more pages than I could find to tell you about them all. I wrote in an earlier chapter about the problem that I had with a strong independent spirit. Perhaps I inherited it from my father who was a "fixer," or perhaps I developed this stubborn independence through having to fend for myself at such an early age. Whatever the reason, I have written earlier that God has had to deal mightily with me to bring me to the place where I look to Him for His leading and direction **before** rushing out on my own. I have found myself in deep water more times than I would like to tell you, just because I failed to *"wait on the Lord"* (Psalm 27:14) for His provision; His solution; and His timing. He has promised to go before us, to supply all of our needs, to comfort us; to correct us; to watch us; to help us; to rescue us; to teach us; etc. He is a caring, loving Father that has promised every blessing to His children if we will trust Him. He stands ready to prove that He can be trusted and believed by every child of promise who accepts life through the gift of His Son.

There have been times of severe financial crises where I have been unable to see the possibility of any solution apart from a miracle by God, but He has always proved Himself faithful. Some of these times were caused by my own foolish mismanagement of God's resources. We each seem to have a tendency to get our wants confused with our needs. The Bible says that man does not see as God sees (1 Sam. 16:7-8). When there is a true need in our lives, whether material, physical, emotional, or spiritual, and we cry out to God to help us, He has promised to answer. His answer, however, will be in His perfect timing, and not always in the way that we want it. When I was struggling with the dark skies and frightening probability of being rained out on that afternoon in May, I would have gladly told God how He should answer! But, later when God's miraculous plan was complete, all I could do was stand in awe of Him. I am so glad that He is in charge, and not me! God is never late, and His hand is never short (Isaiah 59:1)! Eventually, we learn to say, "Nevertheless, Lord, not my will, but Thine. . ." (Luke 22:42).

In 1988, I had the wonderful privilege of traveling to Israel with a group from our church to see and walk the land where our Savior walked. As we stood one day near the Western Wall of the old temple in Jerusalem, our Pastor reached down and picked a mustard plant that was growing through the rocks. He broke open the seedpods to reveal the hundreds of tiny seeds that were almost microscopic to the eye. As he held the tiny dark seeds in the palm of his hand he began to share with us the verses from the Bible, where Jesus explains to His disciples why they could not cast the demon out of a man's son. Jesus' explanation to them was:

> *"Because of your unbelief; for assuredly, I say to you, if you have faith as a mustard seed, you will say to this mountain, 'Move from here to there,' and it will move; and nothing will be impossible for you"* (Matt. 17:20).

I still have the tiny black seeds that I brought back with me. Some of them are still hiding in the crevices inside the binding of my Bible. They are no larger than the size of one of the periods on this page. Jesus was teaching His disciples that the <u>size</u> of their faith was not their problem. Their problem was their unbelief. They had chosen not to believe that God could, and would, move beyond the impossible! Great men and women of faith are born in the trenches of **their will to obey**, when the way over the empty space of "the impossible" is not visible to the eye.

I have heard wonderfully exciting accounts from others who have sought God's provision in times of severe crises; times when they were desperate for a lifeboat in the storm. As soon as God miraculously supplies their need through an act of love that only He can provide, their hearts are awestruck with His love and faithfulness toward them.

Now they know that His Word to them is true. Now their faith has grown by leaps and bounds. I have often paraphrased Philippians 4:19 to read this way, "But my God shall supply all your needs, according to His riches in glory (*just in the nick of time!*)" My paraphrase in parenthesis.

We learn faith to trust Him for His protection over us when there is no other way out without His protective covering. We breathe up desperate prayers when we are faced with impossible and fearful circumstances that only He can cover. The Bible offers many accounts of great giants of faith that sought God in desperate circumstances. The Bible tells us that it is impossible to please God without faith (Heb. 11:5-6). This underscores the truth that there is nothing we can do to please the holiness of God within ourselves; it can only be done through faith in the righteousness of Jesus Christ dwelling within us.

God promises that He will always answer when we "diligently seek Him!" (Heb. 11:6). His answer may be delayed, for reasons that only He knows. Sometimes His answer is different from the one that we wanted, but His answer will come, and it will be the one that is best for us at the time.

Many of us suffer physical illnesses from painful health conditions. I have found myself in some of these, as well. God may call on us to exercise strong faith to face and endure extreme physical illness and pain. These can be hard and sometimes confusing times, but God has promised to walk with us all the way through. He will supply unusual and amazing faith to equal the difficult road we must travel. I will talk more about some of these trials in Chapter 7. These are times when we ask God for the faith to remember that He *"will never leave us or forsake us. . ."* (Heb. 13:5). He promises to be there with us through the most difficult circumstances and He will build our faith to match the occasion.

From the moment of salvation, God's grace—His undeserved favor—is applied to each of us as sons and daughters of the King! The issue for any Christian is not to achieve more faith, but to wield the faith that God has given to us, by that faith! Jesus said to the woman healed of an issue of blood after 12 years, *"'Be of good cheer, daughter; your faith has made you well.' And the woman was made well from that hour* (Matt. 9:22). Jesus was not praising her for her production of faith. The faith that she wielded was not from her own doing, it was a gift of God! Jesus was acknowledging her willingness to act on the

133

faith God had given her. The woman believed in the power of Jesus to heal her and when she reached out her hand and took His garment, she acted on her faith. Ephesians 2:8-9 makes it very clear to us that we cannot do anything to work our way to God; that even the faith that we must have to believe in God is a gift from Him.

Jesus commands His disciples in Matthew 10:8-9 to, *"Heal the sick, cleanse the lepers, raise the dead, cast out demons. Freely you have received, freely give."* Yet, we have insisted on keeping our prayer for healing shrouded in hushed secrecy, like maybe only the very deserving may dare ask for such favor from a judgmental God. I have yet to find one that is that deserving of God's favor, certainly not me. No, I believe Jesus meant it when He offered His love and His gifts to us unconditionally. We must learn to believe that this magnificent Savior died for each of us freely and openly. Then, we will learn to ask and believe. . .and trust His answer.

God does not always heal in the way that we ask. I have heard many credible accounts of those, which, through the prayer of faith, have been miraculously healed and restored to health. I also know and have known so many dear and precious Christians who have suffered through terrible sickness and death due to some awful disease or condition. I have participated in prayer sessions where men and women who exercise great faith have prayed fervently for God to miraculously heal, only to find later that he or she had soon slipped quietly into God's loving arms. We must always remember that our God is sovereign, and we must learn to trust His sovereign will for others, as well as ourselves. He is the only One who knows the future. James 5:14-15 gives instruction to us concerning our prayer for healing. *"Is anyone among you sick? Let him call for the elders of the church, and let them pray over him, anointing him with oil in the name of the Lord. And the prayer of faith will save the sick, and the Lord will raise him up. And if he has committed sins, he will be forgiven."*

Paul tells us that the faith to believe and receive is a gift of God, which cannot be achieved by anything we can do. The more I yield my heart to His Lordship, the more His faith and character is exhibited in my life. To have to achieve on my own enough faith to receive God's gifts or His blessings is an affront to our need for a Savior! God does not bless His children at different levels based on some giant spiritual staircase that we ascend in our growth. This is humanistic thinking and not of God!

By the world's standards, I should have had a serious problem believing God. I have read in so many books of how a person's faith is related to parental trust. It really takes emotional dynamite to cause a child to stop trusting a parent, no matter who or what they are! I suppose I felt the effects and the pain of that dynamite that could have destroyed my life, but God, in His matchless love, saw me and called me to be His child. He has demonstrated His love and protection over my life from the beginning, and His faithfulness toward me has never wavered.

Yes, there will be disappointments and trials. Great faith is not an insurance policy that guarantees freedom from life threatening persecution, pain and death. Those who falsely think this is true have never finished the 11th chapter of Hebrews. This chapter speaks of great men and women of faith, who were stoned, destitute, imprisoned and tortured. Some were even *"sawn in two"* because of their faith. These were men and women *"of whom the world was not worthy"* (Heb. 11:38). This is certainly not the prosperity teaching that we often hear about today. God is not some doting parent that is here to serve you or me. What He does promise, however, is that *"in Christ"* we *will have peace* **with** *God* (Romans 5:1), *and the peace* **of** *God* (Phil. 4:7), that will guard our hearts and minds in the midst of any trial or circumstance that may come our way.

— The Big Picture —

The topper, of course, is His promise to us in the Gospel of John: *"And I give them eternal life, and they shall never perish; neither shall anyone snatch them out of My hand. My Father, who has given them to Me, is greater than all; and no one is able to snatch them out of My Father's hand. I and My Father are one"* (John 10:27-30).

Once we learn the true perspective of the great all-powerful God of the universe, our desire is that our lives will serve and please Him in all of our ways. God has laid eternity at our feet and the road from here is filled with surprises and joys deeper than anything our hearts can imagine

7

"The Bridge Over the River, Why?"

— The Bridge of Adversity —

— Allegory —

The path, once easy and bright with promise, has suddenly become dark and covered with a thick fog that penetrates the landscape with uncertainty and change. Each step now seems hidden and dangerous. The bridge, visible in the distance, spans a steep and treacherous ravine filled with cliffs and jagged rocks.

The gnarled and twisted base of the bridge quakes and heaves in the wind with strange almost audible moans that cry out for relief. Railings, dried and splintered by the winds of time, hang by rusty nails from broken posts. The old girders, once strong and straight, rise above their gray wind-swept pillars like outstretched arms of pain, as if warning of danger ahead.

Relentless, howling winds assault the bridge uprights like accusing hungry predators seeking to steal and destroy. The remainder of light has now been squeezed from the horizon, leaving no hope of vision beyond the bridge.

Hopelessness and fear grips the heart, weakening any resolve to continue. The storm around the bridge seems to intensify as though strengthened

by a sense of victory over another weary traveler. An unutterable voice from deep within the spirit screams a desperate question into the wind —
"Why must I travel this bridge?" "Why me?"

"The Bridge Over the River, Why?"

— The Bridge of Adversity —

"But we have this treasure in earthen vessels that the excellence of the power may be of God and not of us. We are hard pressed on every side, yet not crushed; we are perplexed, but not in despair; persecuted, but not forsaken; struck down, but not destroyed—always carrying about in the body the dying of the Lord Jesus, that the life of Jesus also may be manifested in our body" (2 Cor. 4:7-10).

Pain and tragedy touches all of us at some time or another. A few years ago, one of the worst tragedies that the world has ever seen occurred in Southeast Asia. A deadly tsunami spawned by one of the strongest earthquakes of our time swept away thousands of men, women and children in its crushing waves. In its wake, it left unbelievable destruction, disease and pain. Mothers watched their children snatched from their arms by the force of the raging water. Husbands and fathers were left broken and dazed with the tragic realization that their world had been washed away. Children playing on calm beaches or in the safety of their homes were snatched away in the torrent. Since then, hurricanes; tornadoes; sickness and devastation have swept across the landscape leaving the world breathless with questions.

The world wants to know "Why?" Religious leaders around the world continue to debate this question of "Why?" Why would an all-powerful God allow so many innocent people to suffer such devastating tragedy?

At some time or another, we each seem to have our own personal "tsunami"; a time when a wave of unexplainable proportion seems to wash over our lives, taking reason and predictability from our grasp, and leaving only "Why's" in its wake.

Heartaches can be the painful consequences of our own actions, but very often a tragedy can fall across our life that does not seem to have a reason or a cause. We are a created people with a thirst for answers and the "how's" and "why's" batter our thoughts and emotions with a driving need for answers.

These are baffling times in our lives. When we find ourselves facing one of these difficult times, the response that inevitably rushes forth from our thinking, if not our lips, is. . .

"Why, me, Lord?" "What did I do to deserve this?"

We begin this life by battering our parents with the "Why's," from the time that we begin talking, and we continue in our quest for answers to life's questions for as long as we breathe. Until we come face to face with Jesus Christ and accept Him as Savior, most of us do not know that God has provided mankind with a guidebook that will teach us how to walk in peace through the difficult circumstances of our lives. This book, The Bible, gives us an historical account of God's working in the lives of men and women since the beginning of creation. Within its pages we learn of the character of God and the ways that He has chosen to be involved in the personal lives of men and women. We find direction on how He wants us to live, along with practical reasons and examples that we can follow in our quest for a successful and fulfilling life. Answers to life's deepest questions are revealed within its pages. The amazing thing is that these answers are just as relevant today as they were thousands of years ago when God inspired men to write them down so that you and I would have them to live by today. The Bible tells us in 2 Timothy 3:16-17 that, *"All Scripture is given by inspiration of God, and is profitable for doctrine, for reproof, for correction, for instruction in righteousness, that the man of God may be complete, thoroughly equipped for every good work."* These verses go on to tell us that God uses His Holy Word, the Bible, to equip and teach us how to live the way He wants us to live in this world.

We also read in the Bible, that man is stubborn and willful and intent on going his own way. Isaiah 64:8 says, *"We are the clay, and You our potter; And all we are the work of Your hand."* Sometimes, however, the clay gets marred in the hand of the potter and has to be made again into another vessel (Jer. 18:3-4). God has a perfect and unique design for each of us and He is the only one who knows what it will take to perfect that plan.

Because of His great love for us, God may allow circumstances and struggles to touch us that are painful and confusing at the time that we are going through them. Sometimes, when the struggle is over and we have climbed onto the safety of the other shore, we may be able to see and understand the reasons. There are other times, however, when the road is so difficult and painful that we may have to wait until we see Him face to face to know the answer to our "Why's."

Perhaps this great heartache and trial is caused by a mistake in judgment or a stubborn insistence on doing what we want to do instead of obeying God's direction. Even though these times are caused by regrettable circumstances, I have discovered that God takes our mistakes and turns them into times of correction, leading to brokenness and growth in our lives.

At other times, a baffling series of events seems to arise out of nowhere, stifling our senses and leaving us searching for reasons and causes that are beyond finding out. When this happens, the dimensions of our world seem to cloud over and our focus narrows with a new and painful perspective.

Are these struggles in our lives mistakes? It is difficult for us to believe that a loving God would allow bad things to happen to good people. When they do, we are tempted to judge God as "unfair", perhaps not with our words, but maybe with our thoughts. We expect God to be higher than the heavens; always and only acting in a "Godly way"; but this "Godly way", if examined, seems to be **our definition** of what His response should be. . .not His. His plan for our lives is so much higher than our reasoning that we must learn to trust Him to know what is best in every situation. . .not just the ones that make sense to us!

We may even have the mistaken idea that God only allows blessings to touch His children. If we are completely honest about our thoughts, we think of God as a wonderful benefactor sitting in heaven with only one purpose: to "protect and serve" Christians! No wonder our Christian lives are like seesaws. . .*drifting with every wind that blows*. Yes, God does bless us, but there are times that we do not understand, when the storm clouds blow across our lives causing us great pain. These are the times when we must learn to cling to Him in complete trust. Then we learn that He will be there with us in the storm.

One of the most important truths that we must learn about God is that He is sovereign (Eph. 1:21-21). There is nothing that gets past Him! The Bible tells us that His eye is always on His children (Psalm 33:18)! Most of all, I have learned that He is committed to growing His children into pure and holy vessels fit to mirror the glory of Jesus Christ to a lost world. The pain that we endure, though often intense and grievous, may be allowed to refine a purity and beauty in our lives that can only be released through the heat of struggle.

There have been many deeply painful struggles in my life. I have already shared the years of separation and abandonment that I endured as a small child. These lonely and hurtful years left many deep scars and painful memories that threatened the hope of joy and trust in my child's heart.

After the move to Colorado, we built our dream home on the side of a mesa overlooking the breathtakingly beautiful Boulder valley. Behind the city with the red tile rooftops that defined the buildings of the University of Colorado were the magnificent snow capped mountains and canyons that emptied into the valley below. From the wooden deck that spanned the back of our new home, the panorama of beauty took my breath away. The crystal clear days and evenings with the twinkling lights of the city at our feet seemed like we had entered a secret place that the rest of the world had not yet discovered.

The years that followed, however, brought with them a time of struggle and heartache. A good marriage does not just happen like in the storybooks where the characters always "live happily ever after". A good marriage takes commitment and sacrifice on the part of each person, and still. . .there will be struggle. But, when two people live in two separate worlds spiritually, the struggle can be painful for each partner. It is difficult to write of the times and events that occurred during these years, but perhaps some of my experiences are necessary to share how the stubborn choices that we sometimes make will reap heartache and conflict in our lives for many years to come.

I knew in my heart that my husband was not a Christian before I married him, but I was so intent on having and doing what I wanted, that God's warning to my heart went unheeded. I wanted to be married to this handsome and charming man that every other eligible woman in my hometown wanted. Sometimes stubborn insistence on going our own way results in consequences that cause us great pain and suffering. However, God, in His love for us as stubborn and wayward children, will usually take our wrong choices and use them for our certain good and His glory. The certain good that I am talking about here is characterized as the intense purifying process of fire! **God loves us and turns our foolish choices into opportunities to burn off the stench of the world that we insist on carrying with us into His land of promise.**

Now that I had given my heart back to God, I began to spend long hours searching the scriptures to learn all that God had to say about marriage. I was intent on obeying, not just the letter, but the heart of God's Word for a wife and mother. In the beginning of my marriage I had the foolish idea that *I* could change my husband! God designed women with a strong nurturing instinct that is healthy and vital for our families, but when combined with the push and pull that some of us seem to have in abundance, this can become an issue of *control* that can easily spin **out-of-control**. I could spend the next 10 pages on why God insists on a wife's submission to her husband as her head (Eph. 5:22), and a husband and wife to one another (Eph. 5:21, Phil. 2:3). This is another example in my life where I had to learn to obey God, **because God said so!** God says that *"obedience is better than sacrifice"* (1 Sam. 15:22), and each Christian must learn that whenever God gives emphatic instruction to us in His Word, we must obey whether we understand it or not!

While searching the scripture for God's direction for me as a Christian wife, one of the first verses that I found was in 1 Peter3:1, *"Wives, be submissive to your own husbands, that even if some do not obey the word, they, without a word, may be won by the conduct of their wives."*

It is important to note that this verse says, *"**may be** won over."* Like so many Christians, I interpreted this verse to mean that if I became the kind of Christian woman and wife that God wanted me to be, then my husband would surely be won over to Jesus Christ. I have heard pastors and Bible teachers use this verse as an encouragement for women who were married to unsaved husbands, and in fact, I have used it myself. The likely deduction for a Christian is that when a man sees the beauty of Christ in his wife, she is then more attractive and winsome in every phase of her life, thus making her life with Christ irresistible to her spouse! This leads to the likely judgment that if her husband is not drawn to Christ, there must be something wrong with her walk with Christ. I have heard couples give testimony that the beauty of Christ in their spouse did, indeed, lead them to salvation in Christ. But, I also know that the misinterpretation of this verse has caused many women to be wrongly judged by themselves, or others, because their spouse chose not to turn to Christ.

The beautiful Christian spirit of a godly woman **may** attract her husband to Christianity, but it cannot guarantee that he will make the choice to receive Jesus Christ as his Savior (1 Cor. 7:16). We must be careful not to judge a woman, or a man, if their spouse chooses not to accept God's offer. God has given to each of us the right to choose. This is why God's Word gives careful instruction to the Christian not to be unequally yoked together with an unbeliever (2 Cor. 6:14).

This directive for a Christian is supposed to be obeyed before the marriage. The time to be careful to obey God's warning here is while a relationship is still in the "Hello, how are you?" stage. When a young person receives Jesus Christ as Savior and makes the decision to follow Him in everything that they do, they have already committed themselves to the **decision not to date an unbeliever**! It is a dangerous thing for a Christian to toy with the world's standards, when we know that it will only bring confusion and heartache. If you leave that door open, the enemy will bring along the best that the world has to offer, and he, or she, will probably fulfill every heart pumping characteristic that you have listed on your **"MOST WANTED"** list.

Very often, however, a Christian will become concerned about these verses **after** they are married, or perhaps, after one of them has become a Christian, and the other partner has not. This verse then falls in the shadow of the fact that they are now "one flesh" (Matt. 19:5-6) before God. It would be wrong before God to dissolve the marriage because they are unequally yoked. As I have already shared, God is able to work miracles of love through the Christian partner toward the unbeliever.

The suffering that my family would endure in the years to come was severe and very costly to all of us. But these times of intense fire and trial drove me to the foot of the cross and often left me broken and helpless at God's feet. There in my helpless state of brokenness before God's throne, I found His presence and His touch more beautiful than anything the human spirit can imagine. There I discovered the perfect peace and power to live in God's strength alone.

When two people attempt to live together in harmony as a married couple, it can be very difficult if they live in two different worlds spiritually. Often the one who is a Christian in "name only" becomes confused by the zeal for fellowship with other believers and Church activities that seem to make *no sense*. My husband struggled against even the remotest idea that he should ever need anything more than an outward appearance of Christianity. He became less and less interested in presenting a façade of Christianity that went beyond a sometime

143

attendance in Church. It was hard for him to understand why anyone had to go so far as to live all of the time with an image that he saw as unnecessary. Later, as our children began to be active in Christian activities with young people from church and other Christian organizations, he grew less and less interested in the level of participation that this required of him in his daily life. His chosen lifestyle was challenged by what he saw as "extreme and unnecessary" behavior on the part of his family. It often becomes difficult and aggravating for an unbeliever to live with a Christian because of what the Bible calls, a convicting "aroma" of Christ in the Christian's life. *"For we are to God the fragrance of Christ among those who are being saved and among those who are perishing. To the one we are the aroma of death leading to death, and to the other the aroma of life leading to life"* (2 Cor. 2:15-16).

This, along with circumstances and frustrations in the workplace that disappointed and challenged him, left him reeling as he tried to hold on to a his changing world. This was painful to watch, but any solution I dared to suggest that pointed to his need for a Savior, was quickly avoided and dismissed.

— <u>The Christian is not Exempt from Trials</u> —

There are many shapes and sizes to the struggles that we each encounter, but one thing is certain, not one of us is exempt! The circumstances may be different for each of us, but we all, at some time in our journey, must walk through the valleys and the shadows. Jesus says in John 16:33, *"These things I have spoken to you, that in Me you may have peace. In the world you will have tribulation; but be of good cheer, I have overcome the world."*

*"In the world you **will have**. . ."* leaves no doubt that at some time or another each of us will suffer from some type of trials. However, Jesus says that we can have peace even when we are going through this tribulation. The New King James Version says to *"be of good cheer. . ."* because He has overcome the world. There have been times of desperate struggle during my life when I have found it very hard, indeed, to be cheerful! Then I learned that being cheerful and being of good cheer were two different things. The term, "good cheer" means a state of settled joy and peace knowing that God is in control of our lives personally, and that the whole of our lives is resting in His hands.

The difficult time that we are going through, may sap our emotions and strength and leave us hurting and weak, but we still know that He is able to keep us (2 Tim. 1:12) in the middle of the storm! I would learn in the middle of some of the darkest struggles in my life that I could surely be of good cheer, because He has overcome the world! That "good cheer" is, of course, dependent on our understanding of the last part of the verse, that He *has* overcome the world! Until we fully understand this. Until we get our eyes on what He is doing in the eternal, we will have difficulty walking in this place of settled peace and joy that His "life in us" has provided.

Most of us have read about the refining process of gold. This is such a descriptive picture of how God uses His refining process to burn off impurities in our lives. The gold is melted with an intense heat that causes the impurities to rise to the surface. Then the impurities are skimmed off, leaving a pure gold, of very great value. We all wish to be pure gold, but none of us wants to have to suffer the intense heat of the refining process in order to get there. I have never heard of anyone who willingly jumped into God's refining pot and asked for more heat. I have found in my own life that I get a big case of the stutters when I ask God to change me. Perhaps, because I know that there is still much to be done in my heart and God might usher me into another round of His purification process in order to accomplish the task. When the trial is over, however, I can only bow in adoration of Who He is and His commitment to change me. I have learned so much of His love and gentle touch that I no longer fear anything that might come from His hand, not even when He is forced to discipline me for my own good (Heb. 12:10-11).

Not all of our painful times are because of discipline, or even because of the need for change in our lives. Some of our struggles just do not seem to make sense. These are the times that our trust must rest in the One who does know the "Why's." If you have trusted your life to Him, you know that He can be trusted to *"work all things together for your good"* (Rom. 8:28)! When the world cannot understand, we have the assurance that everything that touches us is in His hands, and for our certain good. He will see us through the worst times and He will be there to carry us when our strength is gone and the way is no longer visible in the darkness.

— <u>God May Want to Show Me My Own Heart</u> —

So often in trials of my own, I have learned that God sometimes allows testing and trials in my life to reveal to *me* how I will respond. Perhaps I need to see my own heart. God may use these times to show me that I am stronger than I thought I was, or that I need to grow in a specific area. Sometimes they show us that we have moved away from God, and we need to run back under His protective wings! God always knows us much better than we know ourselves. I have often assessed the strength and intent of my heart in one way, only to find out through God's testing process that it was much different than I thought. How can I face the hidden things of the heart and allow God to deal with them, if I deceive myself about what is really there?

Since the fall of Adam and Eve in the Garden, men and women have been set on going their own way. From that fateful day forward, man has inherited a sin nature centered and focused on self. This self-centeredness is the opposite of holiness. If we persist in living a life of self centeredness, God may allow a unique set of drastic circumstances to test us. This can be very painful, but will yield life-giving fruit in our lives. I have heard so many testimonies of those who like myself, have walked through deep water and suffered agonizing heartache, only to declare praise to a loving Savior Who loved them enough to allow the storm. In the last chapter I shared how God revealed to me wrong attitudes that I had hidden away in my heart regarding faith and healing. Even though we have many issues settled in our head, sometimes we need one of God's special "spot lights" to show us what we really have hidden away in the deepest part of our thinking. As He walked me through my wrong thinking, I was surprised to see my own heart.

God never meant for us to "tough it out" as we face trials. He has provided His strength for these times as well as the good times. As we learn to lean on His strength, rather than our own, we will begin to grow up as mature Christians. Our wise Father in heaven will often allow us to repeatedly fail in our own stubborn efforts, until we fall on our knees and ask for His strength to withstand. His strength has always been there for us, but until we learn to surrender our willful struggle to "do it our way," we may continue to suffer defeat in our own efforts. Paul says that he pleaded with God three times to remove his "thorn in the flesh," but God's answer to Paul was, *"My grace is sufficient for you, for My strength is made perfect in weakness"* (2 Cor. 12:9).

I read and agreed with this verse many times, but until I was faced with a desperate circumstance that I could not solve myself, I did not really receive it deep in my heart as an anchor of my life. I believe that we are all "learning challenged" as God's children. Why else would God allow us to run into so many brick walls that we cannot possibly scale without His help? When I discovered that God's strength really is sufficient in any circumstance, no matter the size of the giant I am facing, His peace flooded my heart and became a cornerstone of my everyday life.

Paul went on to say in the next verse *"For when I am weak, then I am strong."* He had learned that when he lay down his own abilities and strengths, then Jesus living in him was able to be completely in control of his life and would be victorious. The strength and might of Jesus could then flow through him in power and authority. Otherwise, the world only sees a watered down version of Christianity that has no power. I had to learn that my victory over a trial was not dependent on my strength and ability to withstand the giants in my life.

— Trials Correct My Vision —

Another important reason that God has allowed me to walk in the shadows of trial is to correct my vision. After we have been Christians for a few years, the magnificent miracle of salvation may begin to fade in our vision, and we tend to develop a kind of spiritual myopia. Our vision narrows until we begin to focus only on **our own needs** instead of God's kingdom and what He is doing in the "big picture." The experience of having to lean so heavily on God for His strength in the middle of a trial will always force us to **see Him in the darkness**. The tiny flame of a candle is barely noticeable in the light of day, for we really do not need its light, but when intense darkness melts away the light, the little flame from the candle becomes more valuable than anything else in the world.

— Trials Remind Us of our Need for God! —

Before we will turn from the world and all of its glitter, we must first see our **need for God**. There have been times when my death grip on the world has been so tight that it has taken times of desperation

147

to cause me to let go of the world in order to reach for Him. Until we really discover how much we need God alone to keep us from our own sinful and stubborn tendency to self-destruct, we will never allow Him to change us into the mature men and women that He wants us to be.

Most of us have read in the Gospel of Matthew about Jesus and His disciples when they encountered the violent storm on the Sea of Galilee (Matt. 8:25-27). Jesus had retreated to the boat to rest because He had just finished teaching the Sermon on the Mount. While Jesus slept, a terrible storm came up with waves that were higher than the boat and the disciples were terrified.

Jesus always teaches us how to walk through the storms of life by showing us how to walk with Him in the middle of those storms! If He had pointed to the storm from the shore and told them all about the strength and power He could give them, they probably would have listened and nodded and then, like me, would have to be told again and again. But to show them first hand in the middle of the storm became a lesson they would not forget. Now, they knew that His strength and power was stronger than the storm! This is so very similar to the storm that we experienced with the Garden Tea in the last chapter on Faith.

I believe that the evolution of events that occurred in my life during the painful periods of adversity was used by God to release me from the bondage of my stubborn self-willed independence. My hands and heart needed to be pried from the death grip that I had on my own self sufficient need to run my life "my way". No matter how many times I failed, I just knew that the next time would work! I was a self-proclaimed fixer!

The intensity of my husband's struggle seemed to increase dramatically. Many difficult changes began to occur in his job and in the nature of the way large companies had to adjust in the changing world of sales. He had enjoyed the old way of securing his customers loyalty through an almost seductive style of charm and entertainment. This was, at one time, an effective and even winsome approach to sales. Now, this world of sales, with its whimsical rules for success, like an unfaithful and flirtatious lover, was beginning to abandon him. I watched as he frantically screamed at the quickening pace of his changing world to "Stop!"—But, it would not. Because the giant that he faced was unapproachable and allusive, he began to lash out at those within his reach. He felt increasingly helpless before the giants that threatened his image of success.

I had started teaching Bible classes on marriage and home life while living in Kansas City and found that women were desperately seeking God's direction for them from His Word. During these changing times of the late 70's Christian women were being bombarded with confusing and conflicting messages from the world regarding their responsibilities as wives and mothers. The Bible was being challenged as outdated and irrelevant for women and God was using these classes, and others, to provide spiritual clarity in all of our lives. As women, we learned together how to be obedient to God and His Word while walking in Calvary Love. As I walked through these lessons with them, even in the midst of my own conflict, my heart was strengthened with the truth that I taught. I learned what it meant to honor my husband— not based on his behavior or who he was, but **because God said so**. Ephesians 5:33 says, *"Nevertheless let each one of you in particular so love his own wife as himself, and let the wife see that she respects her husband."*

I was fascinated by the fact that God spoke to the husband about loving his wife. . .*but* He spoke to the wife about respecting her husband. I was a little baffled by this until I read somewhere that God was speaking to each partner at the heart of their spouses need. The very top of the list for women is to be loved and cherished by their husbands. The very top on the husband's list is to be honored and respected by their wives. . .or anyone else. This is the way we were designed by God. The fly in the ointment, however, is the fact that men find it much easier to offer respect than love, and women would much prefer to offer love than respect. Each partner finds it difficult to understand the problem with the other. This is a result of the stubborn sin nature that selfishly rears its ugly head to withhold what the other needs and wants. The good news is that God will, and does provide the power to "see and understand" the needs of the other, and the will to obey.

I sought with all my heart to make these words a guideline for my life and I spent many hours in tear soaked prayer before God praying that He would give me His strength to obey them. There are many verses in the Bible that speak to women about their responsibility toward their husbands, but this one truly seemed **impossible for me**! This was one of the worst "Yeah, buts" in my whole life.

"Yeah but, God, you don't have to live with this man!"

I searched for the "ifs" in this verse, and others that spoke to wives, but there were none. God did not say to me that I had any other option but to *"love and honor him; to esteem him; to admire him exceedingly!"* (quoted from the Amplified Version of the Bible.) All that I had learned about being "dead to me, and alive in Christ" — was severely tested. This is when I learned that the impossible was **only possible** for Jesus as He remained enthroned in my heart. Jesus said, *"The things which are impossible with men are possible with God"* (Luke 18:27).

I hasten to say that I failed so many times! I had a favorite crying and praying spot in my backyard down by an old cottonwood tree, overlooking an irrigation ditch that ran along the border of our property. The lot was large and dropped off in the back with fields and open grazing land beyond the ditch. The majestic Colorado Rockies was a beautiful and quiet backdrop that rose in the distance like a protective shield from the world's questions and prying eyes. This place became my safe harbor where I talked and wept out loud to my Father in heaven. There, I confessed the many failures, the many times that I did not respond in love; the many times that I had lashed out at my husband in my frustration and anger! There, I confessed my need for Jesus to forgive me and change me into the woman that He wanted me to be. There, He touched my heart with His healing forgiveness and His restorative love time after time. There He received endless prayers of praise for His goodness and mercy toward such a stubborn and difficult child! There He met me and loved me and grew me in the middle of my pain! During those years, I spent long hours sitting on the old stump that had been placed under the shade of that tree, weeping and pretending to look at the scenery beyond the fence. There my Father loved and refreshed me in His strength and presence.

— Trials May Be A Wake-Up Call From God —

My husband seemed to be filled with anger and frustration that soon began to chip away at the emotional stability in our home. We have the idea that our behavior only impacts our own lives and we either stand or fall alone. Nothing could be further from the truth. Everything that we do seriously impacts the lives of others around us, especially our families. When one suffers, all suffer. The pain and heartache of God's discipline always affects the rest of the family as much or more than the one at the center. Every right or wrong decision that we make sends a ripple effect throughout the rest of our family. Some of them may cause shock waves for generations to come.

God is long-suffering and patient toward us. He will approach us with His goodness first, trying many different ways, and through the loving touch of many people, to draw our hearts to Him. The Apostle Paul tells us in his letter to the Romans that *". . .the goodness of God leads you to repentance"* (Rom. 2:4).

When the goodness of God fails to touch a heart, then He will use other means to get our attention. Before I fully understood this great love of God toward us, I wondered why so many testimonies seemed to include periods of intense struggle prior to a life saving conversion that dramatically changed a life. That is the persistent love of God that will not stop until a heart turns and surrenders before the cross of Jesus Christ. It is important for us to remember that God *always has the outcome in mind*. Once we have tasted God's love in a personal way, then our prayer becomes, "Lord, don't let me go my own way! Do whatever it takes to keep me close to You!"

The pain and turmoil in our home increased until we were all weary and exhausted, trying to find a solution within ourselves and yet, learning to lean heavily on God for a solution. When we are in the middle of such a great struggle, it is very difficult to stand back and get the full perspective. When the water is this deep, and the battle is long, sometimes all we can do is cry out to God to keep us. I remember trying to pray through my tears, but there were times that all I could do was moan and sob with the agony of a broken heart. Then, I remember time after time, collapsing on my knees before my Savior as He once again and again, showed me the Cross.

Finally, without more explanation of details, I will say that our home was broken; hearts were shattered; and my marriage was dissolved. It is so easy during a time of great pain to allow the intensity of that pain and struggle to destroy our perspective of the Savior and His purpose for our life. If we will stay at His feet and allow Him to comfort us, He will begin to give us His strength for that moment and then the next. . . Rarely will we get an explanation from Him, but the strength and trust that His presence builds in us will mold us into a person of character stronger than we could have imagined in a lifetime. Our tendency in the middle of our hurt is to try and fix blame on another, but our Father in heaven will patiently and slowly, yet persistently, show us the Cross. . .until we finally see Him looking down with His amazing love and forgiveness. When I look full in the face of my Savior on that Cross. . .I don't see "blame" in His eyes for my sins. I only see love and forgiveness. How can I turn and do any less for those who have caused me hurt and pain?

— **The Heart Needs Time to Heal from Severe Pain** —

There, at the cross of Calvary our anger; our demand for justice, when released into the heart of God is dissolved by His great love. When the pain is so great, it will take time to be able to move back from the precipice before we are able to apply God's magnificent love to the big picture. There at the Cross, God's great Love, and God's great forgiveness, was eternally joined and exhibited for heaven and earth to observe. That is why it is impossible to say that we love God, but refuse to forgive. The degree that I stumble over blame and un-forgiveness is the degree of self that remains enthroned in my heart.

When the world has nothing more to offer the child of God but hopelessness, then God leads us to the foot of His cross and there reveals the beauty of His life in us that can only be found alone with Him. In the deep valley of my darkest moment, I discovered the beauty of His face in the heart of the storm. I knew that He loved me before this, but not in the way I came to know Him once the darkness sur-rounded me like a weight that pressed in on my very soul and seemed to squeeze the last drop of the world's light from my vision.

During those years of the deepest trial of a lifetime, I was forced to seek His face and His strength, for I had nothing left of my own on which to lean. Many times I collapsed under the weight of the fear and anger that permeated our home, but Jesus was there! He was there in the eyes of my children as they touched me with their reassurance and love. He was there when I returned home from Bible study one day and found enough money in my pocket to pay off the late payments on the house and the power bills that were months overdue. He was there in the hearts of precious friends who wrote letters that included financial gifts that sustained us when the cupboard was bare. He was there when we arrived home to find that most of our furniture was gone and the house was empty. He was there when a friend arrived with a U Haul full of furniture to fill the living room so that we could list the house for sale. I could go on and on to list the miracles of His love, but the most important miracle of all was the miracle of His presence.

— <u>Trials Change Our Perspective of God</u> —

God gave us the baffling story of Job in the Bible, which demonstrates the frustration and turmoil of human suffering. I still grimace when I read about all of the things that happened to this great and righteous man, but I thank God for his example. As I walked through my own period of trial and pain, I identified with Job in many ways. Job, too, questioned God with the "Why's." God answered Job's Why's with a firm and emphatic explanation of **Who He is**! When we are in the middle of a severe and unexplainable trial, we, like Job, discover that we have possibly forgotten the "big picture" of our Sovereign God and who we are relative to His magnificent design. We become so earthbound and self-centered in our thinking that we may begin to act like a spoiled child before God. Yes, God does love each of us in a personal way and is deeply involved in each of our lives, but we must keep the spiritual horse before the cart, so to speak. Job received a wake-up call from God, which we, too, may need to experience from time to time. Perhaps another look at Job's life would be good for each of us.

When God finished with His response to Job's accusations and questions, Job's response to God was quite different: *"I have heard of You by the hearing of the ear, but now my eye sees You. Therefore I abhor myself, and repent in dust and ashes"* (Job 42:5-6). Job had experienced brokenness as a result of his fierce trial.

Jesus is our example of victory is the midst of the greatest pain and suffering ever endured on this earth, and it was voluntary. He chose to leave His throne in heaven and come to earth with the purpose of suffering unspeakable pain and death for you and me. His death and resurrection offered eternal life to each of us through His sinless blood that was shed in our place. Jesus, by walking through such awful and undeserved affliction and death, earned the right to take our hand and lead us through anything that we could possibly face in this life. Hebrews 4:15-16 says, *"For we do not have a High Priest who cannot sympathize with our weaknesses, but was in all points tempted as we are, yet without sin. Let us therefore come boldly to the throne of grace that we may obtain mercy and find grace to help in time of need."*

Throughout the many years of listening to those who are in the middle of pain and heartache, I learned that God seems to lead me to those who are suffering through similar trials as mine. The truths that

153

God teaches us in our own struggles give us special wisdom that we may then turn and share with someone who may be walking through similar pain (2 Cor. 1:3-4).

The scripture that I quickly think of when seeking to encourage myself or someone else who is going through deep water is usually 1 Corinthians 10:13. I have quoted this verse back to God many times in an effort to remind Him of His promise to me. I am afraid, however, that during most of the difficult years, I misunderstood what God was really saying to me in this passage. *"No temptation has overtaken you except such as is common to man; but God is faithful, who will not allow you to be tempted beyond what you are able, but with the temptation will also make the way of escape, that you may be able to bear it"* (1 Cor. 10:13).

God promises in this verse that He will not allow us to be tempted beyond "what we are able" to bear. Our first inclination when we find ourselves in a grievous trial that we consider greater than we can bear is to accuse God of failing to keep His promise. Perhaps one day when the eyes of our understanding are completely open, we may find that Satan had gone before the throne of God, requesting to "sift us" (Luke 22:31), as he did with Peter, only to be met with an emphatic answer of "No" from God's throne. I believe that these are the times, unknown to us that would have been more than we could bear. Our Father is always watchful and protective over His children. The ones that He does allow must then be the ones that He knows that **we will** be able to bear as we lean on His strength in us.

Most of us mistakenly believe that this means God will open a miracle door of escape **from** the trial. Yes, He could do that if it was His will to protect us like hot house flowers from every possible dip in the road, but then we would be weak and unable to stand strong against the storms of life. In order to withstand the enemy and his deceptive ways, we must grow straight and strong in our spiritual lives, ready for any battle. The "way of escape" that God is talking about is the peace and strength that He will provide *in* our lives in the middle of the storm. This explains the phrase, *"that you may be able to bear it."* He does *not* say, "so that you will **not** have to bear it!"

I have opened my Bible to this verse in 1 Corinthians 10:13 and cried out to God in prayer, even daring to challenge Him with His promise. I have sometimes thought, "This is more than I can bear, and You promised in this verse not to allow that." The intensity of the suffering was, in my opinion, more than I could bear, and I repeatedly reminded God of His promise to deliver me *from* the pain. A prolonged and intense struggle seems to produce in us a sense of desperation for things to be right again. I, too, had to learn that when we abide in Him, His strength in us **is able to bear any trial that we face**, even in the darkest night.

The word temptation in 1 Corinthians10:13, is the Greek word, peirasmos, and means testing, or the "proving by adversity." God does not test us to see **how** we will act, for He already knows how we will act. God often uses trials to reveal to you and me the work that He needs to do in our hearts. He is already there in the future, before we respond. The Bible says that God is omnipotent (all-powerful), omnipresent (everywhere at the same time, past, present and future), and omniscient (all knowing). I did not say that because God knows us in the future, He interferes in our decision of choice. We must be careful to remember that the God-given choice is ours to make in the present. This is difficult, even impossible for our finite minds to understand, except by faith (Heb. 11:1-2).

There is something that happens during those times when you are forced to walk completely alone with Jesus that cannot be experienced within the grand assembly of believers. Perhaps, it cannot really happen for us unless the world drops out of our vision and we find ourselves alone with the candle of His presence in an otherwise darkened room. I feel that my words are not enough to describe these times. But, I also know that apart from the pain and suffering that my Father allowed in my life, I might have never known His sustaining love and tender touch to keep and nourish my spirit when I had nothing else but Him.

My Christian growth made more progress during these intense years of pain than all of the other years combined. I was driven to lean on God's strength and direction to keep and guard my life to such a great extent, that He became the all sustaining anchor in my life.

There are many other kinds of severe trials that we endure and some of them are painful beyond description. I cannot imagine a greater pain than losing a child to the ravages of disease or drugs or some other terrible and unspeakable catastrophe. But, no matter the kind, or the severity, when we call to Him, He will be there. He never sleeps, and His eye is always on His children. Every valley has another path that leads back out into the sunshine, and every bridge has an exit that leads to another shore. Even during times that we doubt that we will ever see the light again, we must rest in the assurance that the brightness of His presence will always light the way.

In 1996 I wrote an article on adversity and pain for Agape Letters, titled "The Cuts Make the Difference." Agape Letters was a newsletter for women that I produced four times a year. At the end of the article, I wrote this prayer:

> *"Yes, Father, we often feel your hand of adversity, stopping us, changing our direction, and usually we don't understand. Almost always, we object; we question your judgment; we even demand relief,—and always you understand that we are human—that we are in frail vessels.*
>
> *And in the darkest times, we cry out to you, and we always find that You are there! If we could reach out and touch your face, we would feel your tears of pain for us as we are allowed to suffer through your purifying fires of adversity."*
>
> *"Teach us to trust You more than we trust our- selves. Comfort us, carry us, but don't stop making us into women of beauty and strength, vessels of honor for your use."*

When the deep waters of trial had receded and the storm was passed, I found many precious jewels left in the sand of my life that I would have never known without the struggle. These lessons, like others that I thought I knew, were indelibly stamped deep in my spirit. These became part of the spiritual fiber that God used to weave His strength throughout my heart and soul. These would bind my love to Him in the eternal.

I learned in the middle of this great pain that the world's most glamorous sparkle is only dust and ashes when seen through the Father's eyes. These priceless pearls of God's heart seem to be found only in the wake of the great storms that buffet and assault our lives. They, like all of the beautiful pearls pressed and assaulted by the sands of adversity and pain, will then reflect the priceless glory of the Master's hand.

"Fear not, for I have redeemed you; I have called you by your name; You are Mine. When you pass through the waters, I will be with you; And through the rivers, they shall not overflow you. When you walk through the fire, you shall not be burned, Nor shall the flame scorch you. For I am the LORD your God" (Isaiah 43:1-3).

❧ 8 ❧

"The Jericho Crossing"
— The Bridge of Battle —

— Allegory —

A deafening roar can be heard from the angry river in the distance as it pounds the steep banks of its borders. The shadowy silhouette of a bridge begins to fill the horizon like a dark curtain across the sky. A chill sweeps over you in the waning light, causing you to shudder with strange feelings of dread.

Great stone towers rise from the sides of the massive bridge like battlements against the dark sky. Loud shrill voices can be heard above the sounds of the river penetrating the darkness with taunting threats of danger to anyone foolish enough to continue. The heavy skies overhead echo with peals of thunder and lightning revealing the outline of the bridge that stands like a fortress silhouetted against the darkness.

A flash of lightning crashes across the sky, illuminating something glistening on the path ahead. A suit of armor, prepared for a great warrior, lies before you as if waiting to be donned for battle. As you approach this unusual sight, your eyes are again drawn to the threat

158

of the great challenge before you. The shadows that stalk you have become more daunting on this part of the journey, and you know that they will not leave willingly. A strange light draws your attention again to the glistening armor at your feet, and your trembling hand reaches down to lift it to the light.

A startling light flashes before your eyes and you move forward to see a sword resting across the path: a sword so beautiful that your eyes can barely focus on the magnificence of its design. As you reach for the handle, a name engraved deep in the blade blinds your eyes. The name smolders with a flame deep within its core that cannot be touched or extinguished. Its magnificent blade has two edges that seem to have been sharpened by the fires of eternity in preparation for the battle ahead. The sword once grasped seems to sing and moan with some eternal breath of power, as though waiting throughout eternity to be released into your hand. It moves with a swiftness and strength that is both astonishing and frightening, but as you lift it overhead, its mysterious power scatters the darkness before you.

The mysterious light moves before your feet as you step onto the bridge, and the fortress, once dark and frightening, now appears exposed and weakened by the power of the One who dressed you with His own armor for this battle. Now you know that the battle was never yours, but His.

"The Jericho Crossing"

— *The Bridge of Battle* —

The journey from Denver to Fayetteville, AR had been exhausting, and we were still only half way there. Our little dog, Mitzi, was an excellent traveler, but was anxious to stretch her legs. We had, at times, driven the 800 miles in one day, but it was a hard trip and we decided to stop at a motel along the highway just out of Wichita, Kansas. There had been no trouble getting a room, but from the moment we walked in, I sensed a strange unsettling feeling. I tried to brush these feelings aside as only exhaustion, but as we collapsed into bed, I was still trying to shake off the sense that something was very wrong in this place. We had stopped for a burger along the way, and as soon as Mitzi was fed and finished her walk, she snuggled down in her bed for the night. After tossing and turning for about an hour, we finally got up and prayed over the room. We usually prayed as soon as we checked into a room, but this time exhaustion had caused us to neglect to do so. As soon as we finished praying for God's covering and protection "in the name of Jesus Christ!" we collapsed in sleep. I shudder to think of the different possibilities of activity that might occur in some of the rooms along the highways, and yet, Christians walk into those rooms and wonder why they cannot rest.

At around 1 am, Mitzi became very restless and began to cry and scratch at the side of the bed. This was very unusual for her, so we knew something was wrong. My husband got up and dressed to take her outside, just in case something had not agreed with her stomach. As soon as they left the room, I went back to sleep. All of a sudden, God woke me from a deep sleep with a command to "Get up and pray for Guy!" This command was spoken into my spirit with such force that I sat straight up in the bed and began to urgently pray for his protection. The minutes seemed like hours as I prayed and listened with my eyes fixed on the door-handle.

Questions raced through my mind, "What is keeping them so long?"

"What kind of evil have we stumbled upon in this place?"

I knew that our God was stronger than the forces of darkness (1 John 4:3-5), and that His watchful eye was on them in the darkness outside the motel.

This is the *mystery of the power of prayer*. God awakened me with the firm and urgent command to partner with Him to release His protection over my husband.

After what seemed like an eternity, I heard the key in the door and he entered the room. In the next few minutes he began to tell me of his frightening experience in the dark shadows alongside the building. He had found an exit door down the hall from our room to take Mitzi out to a grassy spot, but when he returned to the door, it was locked. Standing next to the door was a figure dressed in dark clothing, with a hat pulled down over his face. He said the man's presence struck chills through him, and Mitzi became noticeably upset. He picked her up under his arm and hurried toward the front of the motel to try and find a way to get back into the hallway, but had to go all the way around to the front to find an entrance. He said that there seemed to be something evil about the dark figure standing in the darkness, and he could sense danger in his presence. I told him how God had awakened me with a command to "Get up and pray. . ." and we both knew that there was evil activity in and around this place. We were very eager to be on our way the next morning, and we agreed that, no matter how tired we were, we would never again stop anywhere without first praying over that decision.

When Jesus sent out the 70 disciples in the Gospel of Luke, they returned rejoicing that even the powers of darkness were subject to them in the name of Jesus (Luke 10:17). Then Jesus said to them, *"Behold, I give you the authority. . .over all the power of the enemy, and nothing shall by any means hurt you"*(Luke 10:19).

But then He warned them not to rejoice in this, but rather to rejoice in the most important fact of all; that their names were written in heaven (Luke 10:20).

Yes, there is much evil in the world today. Should Christians walk around in fear? No! But we should be aware of the enemy and always be on guard spiritually. One of the biggest mistakes that we make is to call the forces of evil silly, or say that we do not believe that such things exist. The forces of evil are real and they are present and active in our world.

The Bible has a great deal to say about this world of darkness, and gives us important guidelines that we must follow to be victorious in this war. This enemy hates God and he hates God's people.

Just as God's Word tells us about the different levels of holy angels and their responsibilities and powers, so there are different levels of Satan's fallen angels and their responsibilities against God's plan and His people.

I find the account of the prophet Elisha in 2 Kings 6 very encouraging because it points out to us that the angelic forces of God are present and active around His people—to protect and fight for them.

> *"And when the servant of the man of God arose early and went out, there was an army, surrounding the city with horses and chariots. And his servant said to him, 'Alas, my master! What shall we do?' So he answered, 'Do not fear, for those who are with us are more than those who are with them.' And Elisha prayed, and said, 'LORD, I pray, open his eyes that he may see.' Then the LORD opened the eyes of the young man, and he saw. And behold, the mountain was full of horses and chariots of fire all around Elisha"* (2 Kings 6:15-17).

The enemy has patterned his armies after the armies and forces of God. We are told in the Book of Daniel (Daniel 10:4-21) about the prince over the kingdom of Persia that fought for 21 days against the Messenger of God that had been sent to deliver an answer to Daniel's prayer.

This prince of Satan's army was very powerful and the Messenger told Daniel that only when the Archangel Michael came to help him contend with the prince of Persia, was he released to bring the message to Daniel.

Any successful general in the armed forces will tell you that the gathering of intelligence is a very necessary and effective part of war in order to defeat the enemy. The Christian, too, must prepare for the enemy's tactics, by studying God's Word. We make ourselves vulnerable to him by letting our spiritual guard down, or by stepping outside of God's protective covering when we engage in sinful habits and practices.

Strong words are spoken by Jesus about sin, *"If your right eye causes you to sin, pluck it out and cast it from you. . ."* (Matt. 5:29). Jesus is talking about activities that draw a person into sin. This illustration by Jesus emphasizes the danger of allowing yourself to indulge in activities that will lead you into sin. He is saying that it would be better to be without an eye than to be drawn into activities of immorality or pornography, or some other sin that could destroy the heart. Jesus wants His hearers to see that the real source of sin is in the heart. The Bible says that a man, or woman, will become whatever he or she entertains in their thinking (Proverbs 23:7). When a Christian allows himself to think on a sinful activity or pleasure, the actual activity of that sin is sure to follow. Paul writes in his letter to Timothy that we must flee, or run from, sin. Then, he goes on to say that the way to do this is to *"pursue righteousness, godliness, faith, love, patience, gentleness"* (1 Tim. 6:11). The Bible says that when we participate in sinful activities we give a "foothold" to the devil (Eph. 4:27).

Christians need to be careful not to be preoccupied with the activities of evil, whether out of curiosity, or by entertainment. The enemy will use the thoughts and images that we store in our minds against us when we least expect it. I read a fictional novel while I was in college that I knew was very displeasing to God, but I persisted in reading it anyway. Later, when God began to use me to share the message of truth to women in churches and other places, images of some of the descriptive parts of this novel would pop into my mind right in the middle of a teaching or presentation. Was this a chance coincidence? No! This was a carefully planned opportunity by the enemy of the Gospel to distract me and derail God's message of love to the women present. The hurtful part to me was that I had given him opportunity many years before when I stored this filthy literature in my mind. There are hundreds—maybe thousands of books and articles that fill the bookstores today that glorify the enemy and the "enterprises of darkness". I went into one of the largest book sellers in Denver recently to find a book for one of my grandsons and was overwhelmed by the stacks and stacks of fiction that markets and glorifies the enterprises of darkness aimed at our children. The Bible says that we are to *". . .have no fellowship with the unfruitful works of darkness"* (Eph. 5:11). We make a very serious mistake, indeed, if we shrug off these books as harmless entertainment.

In the past few years the television airwaves have been deluged with programming that glorifies witchcraft and black magic. It is becoming more and more difficult to find a fictional program that does not in some way present stories in favor of this kind of activity. The enemy's purpose is to make the darkness appear as normal—or light. 2 Corinthians 11:14 says *"For Satan himself transforms himself into an angel of light."*

In 1988, I had the privilege of standing at the site overlooking what is believed to be part of the collapsed wall of the city of Jericho. The historical account in the Old Testament (Joshua 6:1-27) of God's command to Joshua to take and destroy the walled and fortified city of Jericho is a lesson for us as we learn to obey God when facing the enemy. God, through His command to Joshua, had pronounced judgment on Jericho because of their idol worship and their great sin. The city's destruction would be a strong message to the surrounding nations, of the power and working of God.

Jericho was a wealthy and fortified city that was filled with strong "men of valor," or fighting men. They had a reputation throughout the region of being mighty warriors. God appeared to Joshua and told him that the Israelites would not fight in this battle. Joshua was told by God to send out 7 priests before the Ark of the Covenant and blow their trumpets of ram's horns one time before the Ark. The fighting men would follow and they would march around the city one time each day for six days. The people were not to talk or make a sound during each of these marches. What a joke this must have been to the enemy as they watched from the top of their walled fortress. On the seventh day, which was symbolic of the covenant between God and Israel, they were to march around the city seven times and blow the trumpets each time. On the seventh time around the city on the seventh day, when Joshua gave the signal, all of the people were to shout with a great shout. God told Joshua that when they did so, the *"walls would fall down flat."* This is exactly what happened (Joshua 6:7-20). This was an important message for the Israelites, and to the enemy! The word went out to the whole region that God was on the side of the Israelites and that He would fight for them! Everyone knew that it was God's victory. They had obeyed God's direction to the letter and faith in God's power and ability to fight for them was born in the hearts of the people. When the walls fell down Joshua and his army obeyed God and destroyed the city and its inhabitants.

How many times in our Christian walk are we faced with a fortified city like Jericho, with high and impenetrable walls that are far too strong for us? The very image of this stronghold strikes fear in the heart and we want to turn and run. But then, our Captain, tells us to stand and face the enemy because the battle is His—He has already secured the victory.

— How do we prepare for spiritual battle? —

What makes an effective warrior for Christ? Most of us think that only super-spiritual giants in the church could possibly stand against the enemies of God. We have heard so many strange and exaggerated stories from other Christians that we are sure that only super-spiritual giants will ever be able to be effective warriors for Christ! The rest of us just have to take the bruises and bashing that the enemy hands out, unless we can find someone that will go to battle for us! God has provided everything we need to face the adversary and expect victory for the battles that face us.

The first thing we usually do, when facing a battle, is to pick up the telephone and call someone that we feel is strong enough to face this foe for us. Perhaps, a prayer warrior, who will pray it into oblivion, or someone who, in the process of praying for us, might come up with a solution that will help us avoid the battle. Yes, we do, indeed, need the prayers of others when we are facing *any* foe, but this does not mean that we are no longer expected to fight in the battle ourselves.

I wonder if God sometimes watches and shakes His head at our attempts to sidestep the training exercise that would prepare us for the real battle that He knows we must eventually face.

When God called to Moses out of the burning bush and told him of His plan to rescue the Israelites from Egypt, Moses probably thought it was a great idea until the chilling 10th verse of chapter 3. God said to him, *"Come now, therefore, and I will send you to Pharaoh that you may bring My people, the children of Israel, out of Egypt"* (Exodus 3:10).

Then came the well-known response from Moses in Exodus 3:11, "Who am I that I should go to Pharaoh, and that I should bring the children of Israel out of Egypt? This was Moses' version of, "Who, me?" After a continued exchange between Moses' objections and God's patient revelation of His intent to use him in a mighty way, God became angry with Moses.

In chapter 4, we again hear Moses' objection: *"But suppose they will not believe me or listen to my voice; suppose they say, '"The Lord*

165

has not appeared to you.'" So the LORD said to him, "What is that in your hand" (Exodus 4:1-2)?

We might be tempted to criticize Moses unless we carefully remember our own fearful objections in the face of impossible odds. We see the enemy coming toward us and we have an instant urge to turn and run. After all, who wants to face such a powerful and dangerous adversary?

I have heard myself use each of Moses' objections many times over the years, and over and over, I have heard God's clear response, "What is that in your hand?" (In other words, "Have you forgotten that I have clothed you with My armor, and that I have placed My two-edged sword in your hand?")

All through the Bible God instructs us to be prepared! God wants an army of ordinary, praying Christians that are armed and prepared to stand and take the ground facing them in the battle for the hearts and lives of their loved ones. That ground might be their marriage; their children; their neighborhood or any other place where God has placed them.

— God has provided everything we need for the battle! —

We would not go out to face a visible enemy unless we were prepared to face him. The problem is that the enemy does not wait until we think we are ready! My husband and I used to sometimes watch old movies on Saturday mornings and I especially enjoyed the old slapstick comedy. Sometimes one of the characters would grab his opponent's coat and yanks it down around his arms so that he had him at a disadvantage during a skirmish. That is what our adversary does to us; he uses the element of surprise and deceit to get in a crippling blow against us when we are not watching. That is why God tells us over and over in the Bible to *"watch and be sober"*.

1 Peter 5:8 & 9 says, *"Be sober, be vigilant; because your adversary the devil walks about like a roaring lion, seeking whom he may devour." "Resist him, steadfast in the faith, knowing that the same sufferings are experienced by your brotherhood in the world."*

— <u>Three rules of engagement to remember!</u> —

There are 3 very important principles that we must be careful to remember at all times for this battle in which we are already engaged.

1. The first principle to remember is <u>to keep our heart free of sin</u> before God—have a clean heart! This may seem like a page from the 1st Grade Christian Primer, but I still find that so many of us forget the importance of making sure that there is no un-confessed or secret sin in our lives. We walk around with something left undone in our heart, like gossip or a lie, or we secretly entertain a sinful thought, and then we wonder why something bigger seems to attack us. Un-confessed sin gives the enemy free access to our lives because we have given him a legal right to attack us. We are out of fellowship with God—our guard is down, and we are sitting ducks spiritually. This is the opportunity for which the enemy has been waiting. The Bible tells us in 1 John 1:9, *"If we confess our sins, He is faithful and just to forgive us our sins and to cleanse us from all unrighteousness."*

When God awakened me in the motel room that night and told me to *". . .pray for Guy,"* why didn't He just do what He wanted to do without me praying? The most important thing for us to see is that God has chosen to join forces with Christians in this battle to defeat sin in this world, and **this battle is joined through prayer**! Christians have the mistaken idea that God is going to do what He wants to do anyway. This plays right into the enemy's hands.

We must consider how hard the enemy works to keep you and me from praying. The hardest thing in the world to organize is a prayer meeting. Sure, the truly faithful will be there, but we seem to need a disaster of huge proportions to bring even the Christians to their knees. The enemy has watched us become so busy that prayer seems to be pushed right off the table on our "To Do" list.

The point is, we can and will win this battle if we pray! But, we will not be able to pray effectively unless we come to God with a clean heart. Psalms 66:18 says, *"If I regard iniquity in my heart, The Lord will not hear."*

2. A second principle that we must remember is <u>to keep our heart humble</u> before God. Pride is sin, but it creeps into our lives and blind-sides us when we least expect it. One of the most dangerous mistakes that we can make in the face of the enemy is to face him with a proud and arrogant heart. We must be careful to remember that our "Captain" *is* Jesus Christ and that <u>all power</u> belongs to Him—not to us! We move against the enemy only when God tells us to, and when our hearts are clean and humble. I did not say mousy—we have no reason to cower before the enemy. The Bible tells us that he is a defeated foe.

    "Yet in all these things we are more than conquerors through Him who loved us. For I am persuaded that neither death nor life, nor angels nor principalities nor powers, nor things present nor things to come, nor height nor depth, nor any other created thing, shall be able to separate us from the love of God which is in Christ Jesus our Lord" (Rom. 8:37-39).

3. The third principle to remember, and perhaps the most impor- tant, is that <u>un-forgiveness toward another blocks the power and the working of God in our lives.</u> This stubborn unwillingness to show forgiveness is a personal affront to the cross of Jesus Christ, where He bled and died to forgive and redeem a sinful and undeserving world back to God. This blatantly says to Satan and his demonic henchmen that we legally want the best of both worlds. The important thing to remember, however, is that there is no "best" of Satan's world. I sincerely believe that most Christians do not even consider the seriousness of their choice to withhold forgiveness toward another. It seems to rest on the shallow plane of simply, "my right to be hurt, and expect restitution"—perhaps, an attitude of "secret punishment" toward another. This "secret punishment" seems to work itself out in open sullen silence or critical innuendoes toward the offending party. The hurt that one feels and is kept deep in the heart then justifies to us the right to withhold forgiveness. In Matthew 5, Jesus is speaking about this important issue,

> *"Therefore if you bring your gift to the altar, and there remember that your brother has something against you, leave your gift there before the altar, and go your way. First be reconciled to your brother, and then come and offer your gift"* (Matt. 5:23-24).

I am often reminded of this teaching when I kneel before God in prayer. I may sense that something is not right in my fellowship with Him, and the Bible tells me in Psalms 66:18, *"If I regard iniquity in my heart, The Lord will not hear."* This is the bottom line of the whole issue! The Bible says that God will not hear our prayer if we harbor or insist on keeping sin in our heart! We must get it straight in our hearts and minds: We are not exempt from God's laws just because we may not know them or respect them! God has given us His Word at great cost to Him.

I have already spent a whole chapter on this issue, but it is deadly for the Christian. Your desire to be used by God in any effective way will be nullified by a heart of un-forgiveness. If you have found that your Christian life has not moved beyond the "Go" mark, it is time to ask God to search your heart. **Un-forgiveness toward another opens the door for crippling attacks by the enemy.** If there is still a problem here, perhaps you should go back and read again the chapter on forgiveness and *give* God permission to change your will to forgive.

These three principles must be carefully watched in our lives, at all times. This is like staying "at the ready" so that we will not be caught off guard.

Then, in Paul's letter to the Ephesians, we are told to be careful to dress ourselves for battle by putting on the entire armor that God has prepared to protect us. In the 6th chapter of Ephesians, we see the pieces of armor that God has prepared for His children. In Paul's letter to the church at Ephesus, he sends instructions to Christians about the adversary that they face, and the importance of wearing the entire armor that God has provided for their protection. To fail to be prepared when facing the enemy leaves us vulnerable to his attack. Paul wrote this letter from his prison cell in Rome where Roman soldiers wearing these pieces of armor, guarded him day and night. The Roman army was the most successful, and battle worthy army that the world had ever seen and each piece of armor was vital for their protection. When

Paul wrote to the church about the dangerous enemy that they faced, he drew an important picture for us today.

> *"Put on the whole armor of God, that you may be able to stand against the wiles of the devil."*
>
> *"For we do not wrestle against flesh and blood, but against principalities, against powers, against the rulers of the darkness of this age, against spiritual hosts of wickedness in the heavenly places."*
>
> *"Stand therefore, having girded your waist with truth, having put on the breastplate of righteousness, and having shod your feet with the preparation of the gospel of peace;"*
>
> *"Above all, taking the shield of faith with which you will be able to quench all the fiery darts of the wicked one."*
>
> *"And take the helmet of salvation, and the sword of the Spirit, which is the word of God; praying always with all prayer and supplication in the Spirit, being watchful to this end with all perseverance and supplication for all the saints—"* (Eph. 6:11, 12, 14-18).

Paul starts out by telling us that our **strength is in the Lord**. We are not expected to face this enemy in our own strength! This passage in Ephesians is like "The Christian's Order Book for Battle." Verse 11 warns us that the enemy is deceitful, and he will use trickery against us. He goes on to describe the different levels of authority in their powerful spiritual realm. But, then, he makes sure that we understand that God has prepared us to face this dangerous foe before us, in the power of Christ.

I believe Paul's warning to us today would sound something like this, "Watch out! Be on your guard, because he will sneak into your life and jump out from dark corners when you least expect him. For this reason, you must be wearing your protective armor at all times. When you are well armed, you will be able to stand and face him confidently."

God's eye is on us continually, and He is faithful to nudge us of impending danger, but unless we are listening and watching, we may miss His warning (Psalms 33:18).

In Ephesians 6:12, Paul tells us that our enemy is not flesh and blood, but "principalities, . . .powers. . .rulers of the darkness of this age. . .spiritual hosts of wickedness in the heavenly places". He is letting us know that this is serious business. Therefore, we must be clothed at all times in the whole armor that God has provided for us (Ephesians 6:13). In this verse Paul makes it clear that we will only be able to withstand the enemy, if we take up the armor.

— The Belt of Truth —

Tighten the belt of truth about our loins. The loins refer to the sensitive area of the back and sides between the hip and the ribs—a tender and vulnerable part of the body. *The "belt of truth"* also holds the sword, which is the Word of God. The enemy will surely attack the one who is lax in tightening this belt of truth. Paul says that the mature Christian will *"speak the truth in love"* (Eph. 4:15). The *enemy loves* to encourage the Christian in "a little white lie" then expose it before others in order to ruin the Christian's credibility and reputation.

There is nothing stronger for a Christian than the spiritual protection, day in and day out, of knowing that he or she has established the habit of truthfulness. Truthfulness produces confidence and boldness in the life of a Christian and is an absolute must if we would dare to engage the enemy. We are warned in many places in Paul's letters to Timothy to be careful to maintain a pure conscience, lest we shipwreck our faith (1 Tim. 1:5-7; 18-19; 3:9).

Another verse warns against the possibility of our conscience becoming seared (1 Tim. 4:1-2). This means that a person's conscience eventually loses the sharpness of conviction when guilty of sin. A pure conscience before God and man is a prescription for health and effective boldness in the face of the enemy.

— The Breastplate of Righteousness —

The breastplate of righteousness guards the heart. The breastplate in the Roman armor covered the soldier's body from neck to thighs in order to protect the vital organs of the body. Righteousness means **right standing with God** by having received redemption through the blood of Jesus Christ. Because of the blood of His Son, Jesus, God the Father imparts the righteousness of Jesus Christ to each one that is washed in His blood that was shed at Calvary. *"But God demonstrates His own love toward us, in that while we were still sinners, Christ died for us"* (Romans 5:8).

This redemption makes us heart healthy, or alive in Jesus Christ. This is a vital piece of the armor that God has prepared for us, but we must take it up and put it on by receiving Jesus Christ as the Savior of our lives.

— The Shield of Faith —

We must lift up over everything the shield of faith. God has provided this protective shield for us, but we must lift it up between ourselves, and the enemy. How foolish it would be to stand before the enemy with darts of accusations and condemnation flying at us from every angle, and not even lift up the shield that will protect us. The enemy comes to us with accusations of sins from our past to try and defeat us. However, the Bible tells us that there is no longer any condemnation before God for these past sins, because the blood of Jesus Christ has canceled the debt of sin against us (Romans 8:1). When we hold up the shield of faith in all that God says about us in His Word, the enemy's tactic fails and we continue to advance in victory. I know many Christians that think that just because they hear the enemy accuse them, this makes it true. We may get accustomed to accepting the arrows and darts that fly toward us and lower the shield of faith. Sometimes, I just stomp my spiritual foot at the enemy and say out loud, "Don't try to fool me again! I know that God's Word says that 'I am forgiven by the blood of Jesus Christ!' I will not be accused by you again!"

Each weapon is vital for the Christian's protection. The enemy will not leave us alone because he is nice, or because he gets tired of bothering us. He loves to see us cower in a corner. The Roman soldiers would dig trenches and fill them with water on their battle lines. The shields were brass covered with leather so that they could soak them in the water-filled trenches to quench the fiery arrows that the enemy would rain down on them from the enemy. Paul says that our shield of faith will quench every fiery attack that the enemy hurls at us, but we must use it.

— <u>The Helmet of Salvation</u> —

The helmet of salvation is the assurance that we are born-again in Jesus Christ, and therefore heirs and joint heirs (Romans 8:17) with Him of all of the rights and privileges of heaven. This settled knowledge protects our head and our mind from the deadly blows of doubt that the enemy would use against us. When a Christian is 100% sure of his right standing through the blood of Jesus Christ, there is no power under heaven that can shake him. The enemy tries to get the Christian to doubt his salvation so that he can attack the mind.

I have a wonderful friend that I deeply love, who fought this fiery dart from the enemy for many years. The root of the enemy's success in using it in her life stemmed from a wounded spirit and broken self-image as a child. She is one of the most beautiful and gentle Christian women that I know, but she struggled for many years with this issue of seeing herself as an heir of His kingdom—based on the blood of Jesus Christ, and not on how good she is today! Today, she is a victorious warrior in God's kingdom.

— <u>The Shoes of the Preparation of the Gospel</u> —

We must put on the shoes of the preparation of the Gospel. The Bible instructs us to prepare our heart by studying the Bible (2 Timothy 2:15). So many women have said to me that they cannot talk to anyone about the Gospel because they do not know the Bible. My answer is always, "It is time that you prepared your heart to be used by God!" I copied Bible verses on small 3" x 5" cards and kept them in the glove compartment of my car. When I drove my children to a practice, or when I had to wait to pick them up at school, I would pull out my cards and work on memorizing key verses in the Bible. 2 Timothy 2:15 says, *"Be diligent to present yourself approved to God, a worker who does not need to be ashamed, rightly dividing the word of truth."* Unless we prepare ourselves with God's Word, we will not be ready to be used by Him. We must be ready to give an answer to each person we encounter (1 Pet. 3:16-18). The Spirit of God prepares their hearts and lives, but we must be ready to tell them about Jesus Christ!

I made an appointment with a new hairdresser a few years ago in an attempt to try someone new. The very first day, she seemed interested in the meaning of my name. She asked me if I knew that it was Hebrew. I told her, yes, but my aunt happened to get it from a novel that she was reading at the time I was born. This opened the door to her Jewish heritage. In the next few seconds, God seemed to speak to my spirit with a direct command, "Ask Me for her salvation!" I quietly whispered a prayer up to God, asking Him to bring someone into her life to share the truth of Jesus Christ with her. Now, I was the one sitting in this chair every week, and yet, I was asking God to send someone else to speak to her about Jesus! Clearly, in my mind, it was not possible for me to lead an orthodox Jewish girl to accept Jesus Christ as her Savior—the Messiah! I thought that I was not knowledgeable enough.

Our conversations grew and deepened until, a few months later, I asked her if she would like for me to make an appointment for her with a Hebrew Christian pastor who could effectively answer all of her questions. She agreed, and on the morning of her appointment we arrived at his church to find the doors locked. He had forgotten. I knew that this girl's heart was ready to accept Jesus Christ as her Savior, and I knew that I could not allow her to leave empty. We sat in my car in the parking lot of the church while she bowed her head and very simply, prayed for forgiveness for her sin and asked Jesus Christ to come into her heart and be her Savior! When our feet are shod with the preparation of the Gospel, it does not matter who we are or how educated we might be, only that the Spirit of God lives and loves in our heart. *He does the rest!*

— **The Sword of the Spirit** —

We must pick up the sword of the Spirit, which is the Word of God. How can I say enough about this piece of armor? First of all, it belongs to the Spirit of God—it is His and He is responsible for using it effectively! However, it is our responsibility to pick up this two-edged sword, by reading and studying the Word of God—by depositing it deep in our spirit. When the Christian spends quality time in the Word of God on a daily basis, God's truth becomes a part of his thinking. You no longer have to hesitate to know the decisions that must be made in any crises. Those decisions naturally flow out of our lives, like breathing in and breathing out.

Jesus, Himself, demonstrated the power of God's Word over sin when He allowed Himself to be taken up into the wilderness to be tempted by Satan. He even gave Satan a handicap: Jesus was physically weak from fasting for 40 days and nights. Each time Satan brought his worst at Jesus, He answered with the Word of God. Not just any verse, but the most appropriate and powerful verse that the Spirit could find to deal with the problem. This is what He will do for us!

I received a phone call one day asking me if I would meet with a group of women from a particular religious group to answer their questions about Christianity and the Bible. My first thought was, "Good heavens, who do you think I am?" My second thought was from God, which reminded me of the verses in Ecclesiastes that says, *"In the morning sow your seed, and in the evening do not withhold your hand"* (Eccl. 11:6).

It was as though God was saying to me, "If you really believe that I can do this through you, you will not be afraid to go."

I agreed to meet with them, thinking that this would be a small group. I knew there was no way I could be prepared for this group, except by the power of the indwelling Spirit of God to field and answer effectively every question they might ask. I was terrified, but I knew that my God was equal to every challenge. Yes, I had taught Bible studies for years, but nothing could have prepared me, out of my own knowledge, for such an encounter. I confessed my inability to face this challenge within my own knowledge, and asked God to supernaturally answer their questions with His truth through me. The living room of the home where we met was full to overflowing with women. I began with prayer, in which I confessed out loud before God's throne that I did not have the knowledge within myself that they needed, but I knew that He did—and that He loved them enough to answer their heart questions. I deferred completely to Him. Hours later, the women with eyes wide with truth—truth that only the Holy Spirit of God could have supplied—reluctantly left the home. The Spirit of God had wielded the magnificent sword of God's Word in a way that astonished me. God has never used me before, or since that day in such a way! All I did was show up! He cannot do that until we pick up the sword in the battle! God's Word says, *"Preach the word! Be ready in season and out of season. Convince, rebuke, exhort, with all longsuffering and teaching"* (2 Tim. 4:2).

— **Prayer** —

And then, we are told in Ephesians 6:18 to persevere in prayer. Prayer is where the action is! When someone is told to persevere, they are encouraged to "hold out," to pursue, or "follow after" God in prayer until God answers, or He resolves the problem. I remember that one of my college professors described it as "stick-to-it-tive-ness." The tenacity to stick with a job until it is finished or completed.

Prayer—powerful, believing, fervent prayer is the battleground of the Christian! The Bible tells us that *"the effective, fervent prayer of a righteous man avails much"* (James 5:16). The word "avails" in the Greek means "to have power," to have the spiritual power to make a difference with fervent prayer. We are told in II Corinthians 10, that the war that we are engaged in is not a physical battle, but a spiritual one—fought in the spiritual realm, with spiritual weapons.

> *"For though we walk in the flesh, we do not war according to the flesh. For the weapons of our warfare are not carnal but mighty in God for pulling down strongholds, casting down arguments and every high thing that exalts itself against the knowledge of God, bringing every thought into captivity to the obedience of Christ,. . ."* (2 Cor. 10:3-6).

Prayer is the Christian's powerful weapon against the enemy's forces of darkness. Jesus has already defeated Satan's power through His death and resurrection, but we must partner with Him to set the captives of sin and death free from his evil kingdom. We do this by agreeing together in prayer. Jesus tells us in the 12th chapter of Matthew that with the powerful weapon of prayer, we can bind "the strong man" and then "plunder his house." *"Or how can one enter a strong man's house and plunder his goods, unless he first binds the strong man? And then he will plunder his house"* (Matt. 12:29-30). The strong man is the enemy that holds us captive. Fervent, persistent, and believing prayer can release his hold on us spiritually.

Our world is filled with thousands and thousands of broken lives that are bound by the forces of darkness through drugs, alcohol, pornography, hurt, incest, physical and emotional abuse—lives without hope of ever being free to choose Jesus Christ and His great freedom.

This dark fortress stands on the horizon taunting the Christian not to even try the impossible attempt to storm its gates. But our Captain, Jesus, bids us to follow Him through the power of prayer, right through the gates of this darkness, and back out into the light of His love and forgiveness, bringing the captives with us. Yes, **it is possible** for the warrior who understands God's Word and the real battle before us. We are all in this battle. If we are not fighting, then we are losing!

Ezekiel 22:30, 31 says that God looked for a man to *"stand in the gap"* on behalf of the people of the land, but He found no one. The consequences in Ezekiel 22:31 are tragic! *"Therefore I have poured out My indignation on them; I have consumed them with the fire of My wrath; and I have recompensed their deeds on their own heads," says the Lord GOD."*

God says that He could not find one man to stand in prayer between Him and the sins of the people. Are we too busy to kneel before God and do battle for our families, our church, our city, and our nation? The tragic changes in our world suggest that we are losing the battle.

God has chosen to partner with Christians in prayer—to work out His will on this earth until He returns! God has called us; filled us with His love; given us written instructions; taught us; armed us with His Spirit; prepared us; revealed the mysteries of His kingdom to us; and we still stand back and say, "I'm just waiting for Him to show me what He wants me to do."

Years ago, when I first began to speak and teach for different groups, I began to notice that many different types of conflict and disturbances began to escalate throughout my home and family relationships as the date of each speaking engagement drew near. I was also plagued by thoughts that began to bombard my mind. These thoughts were foreign to my mind and their shocking content stunned me. I was especially dismayed that such things could even come to my thoughts. I knew that the enemy hated what I was doing, but I was not prepared for such a vicious attack. I prayed continuously for God's protection and His covering, but the attacks on my mind continued. I would pray for the blood of Jesus to wash me and keep these ugly things from my spiritual ears. As the days and weeks went on, I became very discouraged with this vicious attack, and I prayed fervently for God to show me how to fight this powerful adversary.

Then one night, I was awakened at 2 a.m. with a horrible nightmare. I sat up in bed in the dark, terrified with the images that I had seen in this dream. Every detail was cemented in my mind and I was sure that it had been played there by some devil sent to trouble my subconscious and destroy my sleep. I prayed for God's protection and lay awake for some time thinking of the terrible dream. The dream could not be shaken as I went through the following day, and I wondered how much more of this I could stand.

The next night I prayed and asked God's protection over my subconscious while I slept. At 2 a.m. I awoke with the same dream, exactly as it had been the night before. I lay there in the darkness praying for God's protection over me as the ugly details once again played out in my mind. The only difference was this time I was not frightened the way I had been the night before. The next morning, I asked God if this could possibly be a message from Him. I promised Him that if I had exactly the same dream again the third night in a row, at exactly the same time, I would know that it was from Him and I would search for its meaning. Otherwise, I would not entertain any more thoughts of its contents. The third night, I again prayed before I went to sleep, asking God to protect me from anything that was not of Him. At exactly 2 a.m., I sat straight up in bed as if God had thrown cold water on me. Every detail had again played out in the dream as before. The next morning, I began to ask God what He was saying to me through this strange dream.

The setting for the dream was a library with tall shelves of books that were positioned like any large university library. In the center of the library there was a table where a woman sat reading a book. I stood in the back of the room watching her. Then I saw huge evil creatures with wings darting about the top of the room. They were hideous and disgusting, like nothing I had ever seen. At intervals, they would dive with great force toward the woman sitting at the desk. This terrified me as I watched, but it did not seem to bother the woman at the desk. After I watched this sight for a time, I walked over to the woman at the desk and asked her if she was afraid of the horrible creatures that flew through the space around her, narrowly missing her head. She quietly answered, "No, all I have to do is use the name of Jesus—and they cannot harm me!" It was always at this point that I would wake up.

I called a Christian friend of mine and told her the sequence of the dream over the last three nights. She also thought that the dream was from God, and told me that there was an interesting chapter about dreams in Katherine Marshall's book, "Something More."[10] I knew that I had the book and quickly hung up the phone to search for the particular chapter on dreams. The whole chapter was fascinating, but then she explained that when there is more than one person in a dream it usually means that they are both different parts of the same person. Instantly, I knew that this was true of my dream. I was standing in the back of the room watching the woman at the desk, but I was also the woman sitting at the desk. I already knew what God said in the Bible about our "authority in the Name of Jesus," but I was so shaken by the attack, I had failed to apply the powerful solution that I had known about for so long. We must know that the enemy likes to catch us off guard and establish fear in our hearts. Fear paralyzes the quiet spirit that we must keep to effectively face this ruthless enemy!

The Bible says in Philippians 2, *"Therefore God also has highly exalted Him and given Him the name which is above every name, that at the name of Jesus every knee should bow, of those in heaven, and of those on earth, and of those under the earth, and that every tongue should confess that Jesus Christ is Lord, to the glory of God the Father"* (vs.9-11).

From the time that I became a Christian I had been taught the importance of always coming to God the Father through, and in, the name of Jesus (John 14:6).

The next day I drove my daughter to gymnastics practice and had stopped on the way to pick up my mail. I had ordered little booklets for the Bible class I was teaching, titled "My Heart Christ's Home." I waited in the car for my daughter so that I could review the little booklet that I planned to hand out in the class. The booklet starts out by saying that when we invite Jesus Christ into our heart, He enters each room and begins to reside there, making any changes necessary to clean up the house. One of the first rooms that He enters is the "library of the mind." I almost screamed out loud. God had just shown me another part of the dream. He was showing me that demonic forces attack us in our minds. This is what had been happening to me for many weeks, and I was growing weak from the onslaught. The little booklet that had been ordered weeks earlier was planned by God to arrive on that day. God's demonstration of the power in the name of Jesus through the

---

[10] Something More, In Search of a Deeper Faith," Catherine Marshall. McGraw-Hill Book Company, New York. © 1974 by Catherine Marshall LeSourd. P. 101.

dramatic picture video played to my subconscious mind empowered my faith. I could now wield this weapon with absolute authority! We need to remember here that words alone will not make the forces of evil flee. Yes, there is power in the name of Jesus, but that power is used by the indwelling Holy Spirit that wields the authority of the One behind that name. There are many scripture verses in the book of Acts where the disciples were commanded by the Jewish officials not to preach and teach "in the name of Jesus" because of the many people that were being healed, and their lives changed, in that Name.

The enemy's tactics never change, he sees our weaknesses and failures, and capitalizes on them over and over. No, the devil did not make us do it! He can only succeed against us if we let him! He is a defeated foe, and he cannot make us fail. God has provided the victory, the strength, and the armor that we need to break the habits and weaknesses in our lives. We must make the choice to *"walk in the light, as He is in the light"* (1 John 1:7). If we allow ourselves to indulge in sin for a time, it can become a habit that is hard to break. This sin has now become bondage, or perhaps, a stronghold (2 Cor. 10:3-6) of sin. The Christian then needs the help of a pastor or other Christians to help him break this bondage that may have gained a powerful hold on his life. Jesus talks about this in Mark 3:27, Matt. 12:29, and Luke 11:21.

We are told not to fear the enemy because Jesus, by His death and resurrection, has conquered Satan and all of his forces of evil.

> *"When you go out to battle against your enemies, and see horses and chariots and people more numerous than you, do not be afraid of them; for the LORD your God is with you, who brought you up from the land of Egypt"* (Deut. 20:1).

It is important to note that in all of the pieces of armor that Paul names in Ephesians 6, there is not one piece of protection for the back. This is because the Christian is told to "stand" and face the enemy. There is never any need to retreat from him. Jesus has won the victory, and He is our Captain. Paul tells us in Colossians 2:15, *"Having disarmed principalities and powers, He made a public spectacle of them, triumphing over them in it."*

Psalm 27:1 says, *"The LORD is my light and my salvation; Whom shall I fear? The LORD is the strength of my life; Of whom shall I be afraid?"*

When we have done all that He has told us to do, we must stand and trust! There is no safer place for the Christian to be.

> *"You are of God, little children, and have overcome them, because He who is in you is greater than he who is in the world"* (1 John 4:4).

"Covered Bridges
Over Troubled Waters"
— The Bridges of Brokenness —

— Allegory —

T he surrounding countryside is peaceful and pleasant after such an exhausting journey. To one who has encountered so many obstacles, the small covered bridge in the path ahead seems barely noticeable, even unnecessary, for such a small stream of water. Closer inspection however reveals sharp and slippery rocks beneath the water's surface that could easily cause you to lose your footing.

The construction of the bridge is plain and simple to the eye, with rough-hewn boards weathered by the ages. Some stubborn willfulness within you struggles against crossing the arched threshold that frames the bridges entrance. Excuses and objections bombard the mind, like heavy weights that hinder and drag against the heart.

As you step into the bridge's shadowed interior, the walls seem to expand in their depth and width revealing a great room covered with rich tapestries and lush carpets beneath your feet. A magnificent curtain of royal purple velvet hangs against the back of a raised platform at the far end of the room. The contrast of the room's shadows and the brilliant light that escapes from beneath the curtain makes it almost impossible to focus your eyes in these strange surroundings.

A wave of warmth and healing begins to surround you as you stand in awe before the golden stairway leading to an opening in the great curtain. Though your heart is stricken with fear, you are drawn to the mysterious light that escapes from beneath the folds of the curtain. Beautiful letters embroidered in scarlet, glow like burning embers against the backdrop of its heavy folds.

"THE SACRIFICES OF GOD ARE A BROKEN SPIRIT, A BROKEN AND A CONTRITE HEART— THESE, O GOD, YOU WILL NOT DESPISE."[11]

The power of these words sinks deep within the spirit and you stand transfixed before the truth that is revealed to your heart. Awareness of attitudes of pride and covered sin sweep over you, leaving you weak with shame before the brilliance of the light behind the curtain. Once again your heart is awakened to the love that brought you to this little bridge, and you find yourself prone and broken before the One that reached down into **the impossible** and set your feet upon this amazing journey. A rare and beautiful fragrance begins to spill from the light as it swirls about the room permeating everything it touches with a sense of worship. Frozen in reverence, the heart can only groan with an unexplainable utterance of praise for the One that dwells beyond the curtain.

Suddenly you find yourself back out into the sunshine, facing the warmth of the meadow beyond the bridge. However, the heart knows that it has been forever changed by the magnificent encounter within the interior of the old bridge.

---

[11] Psalm 51:17, NKJV

"Covered Bridges Over Troubled Waters"

— *The Bridges of Brokenness* —

Many times over the years, I have heard my lips speak the words, "More of You, Lord, less of me!" That is the heartfelt cry of the Christian who truly desires to walk closer to the Master. This is God's desire for us, as well. The problem, however, is that what most of us really wants is just enough of God to satisfy our "spiritual décor."

The place of Brokenness leads us into the throne room of the King! Only the Savior is capable of constructing this bridge of brokenness that will usher us into His presence. He designed and built it before the foundation of the world, with you and me in mind. During our lifetime, He seems to fashion individual and unique bridges that He places in our path designed to change us and draw us back into this place of brokenness.

When I first met Jesus Christ as my Savior, my heart was so full of intense love and gratitude, that I could not get enough of His presence. Into the emptiness and loneliness of my life, He brought joy, excitement, peace and hope. I remember those days vividly, when the light of His presence entered my drab and hopeless little world. How could I help but love Him? Like the woman who came to anoint His head and His feet with costly oil, I, too, would gladly have done the same. The Master's touch reached out to fill the broken pieces of my heart that had been shattered and ravaged by an uncaring world. The one who has received so much can only lay weeping at the feet of the Savior who reached down to rescue and restore. Where there was pain, there was peace. Where there was darkness, there was light.

I believe that a heart of brokenness dwells as close to God's heart as is possible for us in this life. Such a one has touched the heart of God for he has emptied himself of all that the natural flesh clings to and has chosen to walk where Jesus walked—in complete submission to His Father's will. These are indelible and un-definable moments in the life of a Christian that will forever change and shape his or her life. I have known a few who never seemed to leave this place of brokenness before the throne, and their rare beauty and radiance seem to me to depict a kind of secret elixir, that clings to them like a heavenly garment fashioned by the hand of God.

In Luke 7:37-50, we have the beautiful story of the woman who knew that Jesus was dining at the house of a Pharisee, named Simon. Although she was a woman of questionable character, probably a prostitute, she came and stood behind Jesus weeping. She began to wash His feet with her tears and wipe them with her hair (Luke 7:38). She brought with her an alabaster flask of very costly and fragrant oil, which she broke and poured over the head of Jesus (Mark 4:3-9). When the box was broken, the exquisite fragrance of the costly oil filled the room with an aroma fit for the King of Kings, just as her act of worship must have filled the throne room of God with the aroma of praise. Both were released through brokenness.

When the disciples complained to Jesus about the terrible waste of such expensive oil, He told them a parable about two debtors who owed their creditor a great deal of money (Luke 7:41-43). One of them owed him 500 denarii which was 500 times a day's wages, or about a year and a half's wages. The other only owed him fifty denarii, or about a month and a half's wages. Neither of them had any money to repay the debt, so the creditor canceled the debt for both of them.

Then Jesus asked, "Which of them will love him the most?"

Simon's answer was, "I suppose the one whom he forgave more."

Jesus said, "You have rightly judged."

This woman felt the intense hopelessness of her life and the conviction of her great sin. Her heart was broken in love and gratitude to the One who forgave her so much. There is not one of us that have been forgiven any less, but the difference is that she saw the enormity of her need. The heart of intense need always responds with intense love for the One who stoops so low to rescue one so impossible! **Her response of love was relative to her need.**

Women and teens have expressed to me how terrible it must have been to grow up in a boarding school without a family. Yes, it was hard, but I always wonder if I would have needed Jesus Christ as desperately if my life had been so full of all that life could offer me. I truly believe that as we have showered our children and ourselves with every possible material gratification, we have created for ourselves a society that wants and needs nothing. Then, by ceasing to take the time and effort to attend church on Sundays, we have demonstrated to our families and the world that we do not need God.

As I sat in the worship service at church one Sunday morning, a few years ago, the worship leader introduced us to a new song titled, "We Need You Now!" As we sang, I closed my eyes and began to lift the beautiful words to my Father in prayer. My heart swelled with love as I sensed His presence in the room. There was an overwhelming awareness that He was responding to the heart cry of His people. The words lifted from the large auditorium like a beautiful aroma, and I felt in my heart that my beloved Lord was well pleased. As the service continued, I could not dismiss the realization that my fellowship with God has always been the closest during the times that I have needed Him the most.

At other times, we become distracted by the world, and while the intention of our heart begins with the desire to serve only the Savior, we can still become blind-sided by our own good intentions, and self-sufficiency. When this happens, dullness and spiritual sluggishness become settled in our hearts, and seriously affect our fellowship with God. God warns about the danger of this in His Word. Revelation 3:16, 17 says *"So then, because you are lukewarm, and neither cold nor hot, I will vomit you out of My mouth. Because you say, 'I am rich, have become wealthy, and have need of nothing' — and do not know that you are wretched, miserable, poor, blind, and naked —."*

This is the opposite of brokenness and will never find its way into the holy presence of God. Pride in my own ability to run my life *my way* causes me to cease to lean on Him for my every need. I once heard a pastor talk about how the enemy is content to divert our course just a little, because he knows that this "little" will eventually draw us far away from the Savior.

Very often, God will use one of these bridges, designed and positioned at just the right time and place in our lives, to once again bring us back to the place of brokenness. There have been many of these in my life. Each time, they are perfectly planned, and sometimes they are very painful — but always, they are built from a heart of love. This love will not let me go! God sees the finished product of the life of one of His children, somewhere down through the years, and desires to make us into the person that He designed us to be.

The Bible tells us that sin separates us from God (Habakkuk 1:13). We can dress it up in our mind and make excuses for it, but sin is sin, and it removes us instantly from that place of close fellowship with God. The apostle John spoke clearly concerning this issue in one of his letters to new Christians. *"If we say that we have no sin, we deceive ourselves, and the truth is not in us. If we confess our sins, He is faithful and just to forgive us our sins and to cleanse us from all unrighteousness"* (1 John 1:8-9).

I call these verses, the Christian's bar of soap. Even as Christians, we still sin, but God tells us to confess our sin to Him, and be cleansed. This is not something that we should ever put off or neglect, because with our confession, there is instant forgiveness and restoration in our fellowship with God. When our sin is against another person, or causes harm to someone else, God may require that we confess our sin to the other party or parties involved. Otherwise, division may occur in the family of believers, which can cause a great deal of harm in our witness, as well as great pain to the church as a whole.

I shared in an earlier chapter about one of the early, yet very memorable, incidents of brokenness in my Christian walk. This was the evening that I entertained many of the women in my neighborhood for a "Cosmetic Party." A friend and Christian mentor had been invited with the intention that many of my neighbors would be swept off of their feet by her bold testimony of Jesus Christ in her life. The evening was a wonderful success. Many women's lives were changed and I was thrilled and amazed by the power of this special lady's presentation.

When most of my neighbors left for the evening, I turned to her and with adoration and praise said, "Oh, Helen, you were wonderful!"

Her eyes flashed like lightening as she turned on me. "You get your eyes off me, and get them on Jesus Christ!" she said.

I gasped for air as she refused the flattery and praise that I was sure would please her. After she left that evening, I sobbed in brokenness before my Father in heaven. In that lightening moment, my focus was changed. At first, I felt humiliated before her and the other women that remained in my living room, but later, in the quiet of the darkness on my knees, my heart was re-focused only on the beauty of my Savior and His love. I loved Helen deeply for her jealous love for Jesus that would not even dare to breathe a moment of the praise due to Him alone. This was such an important lesson for me and I shall remember it throughout eternity.

Another incident that vividly illustrates God's perfect timing for one of these little bridges of brokenness in my life involves the memory of something that happened at a weekend retreat for women. We were meeting at a wonderful little rustic Christian camp in the

Rocky Mountains called "Camp Id-Ra-Ha-Je." The name means "I'd Rather Have Jesus," and is nestled in a beautiful Aspen forest west of Denver.

These weekend getaway retreats were, by far, one of my favorite things in the whole world. The Rocky Mountains were breathtaking during the fall, and I loved to share God's exciting truth with women who had put aside the hustle and bustle of the world for a weekend to discover God's love and will for them. Their hearts were always eager and teachable before God, and I counted it a sacred trust to be used by Him in their lives.

As we began the retreat, the air was filled with the fresh fragrance and beauty of heaven, beneath a blue, blue sky and the glistening crispness of a September morning. I had prayed and believed for these women to be touched by God during our time together, and the women had greeted the day with hearts and minds eager to respond to everything God had for them during the weekend.

We were sitting outside for the morning session, which was well under way. I was teaching on the subject of Forgiveness and had just made the statement to the women that "sometimes God requires that we make restitution for past sins," when my heart experienced one of those breathless moments when the Holy Spirit speaks indelibly and clearly to the human spirit. In that moment, God called me to account for a sin that I had long since forgotten during my college career 14 years earlier. I had stuffed any recall of this incident far down in my memory. It did not involve another person, in particular, but it was very serious to God. As I shared in another chapter, even though my college years were beautiful and extremely rewarding, I became infected with the spiritually debilitating virus of "I-ism". By the end of my college career, I found myself far from God. A few years later when God bombarded my life to draw me back to Him, I repented before Him for all of the years that I had strayed far from His will, but I did not remember this particular incident.

Time seemed to stop, as if God pushed the "pause button" at that moment in my life, while He replayed this incident to my heart and mind. I honestly had not remembered what I had done for fourteen years! Why now? Why would God drop this into my heart at this particular time? After all, I was in the middle of teaching His women—for His purpose. My heart was locked into the moment. I knew that I could not continue with teaching until I dealt with the issue at hand. I suggested that the women take a 20-minute break and find a secluded spot in the surrounding golden wonderland to be alone with God. I walked away from the group until I found a secluded spot and fell to my knees before my Father in heaven. I wept over the remembrance of this sin and asked His forgiveness. As I continued to pray, I heard my own words that I had spoken to the women just a few minutes earlier and the Holy Spirit impressed on my heart the need to face this sin from so many years ago.

How could I go back and trouble the college with such a silly thing after all these years?

Why was this suddenly so important to God, —today—at this moment in time?

I begged God not to require this of me, but found no release. Finally, I promised my Father that I would write a letter to the college and confess my sin. I was humbled and broken by the renewed awareness of the incident and wept in repentance before my beloved Lord Who loved me enough to hold me to the highest, even after so many years. Instantly, the heaviness in my heart lifted and I was able to return to the women and resume teaching. God's Holy Spirit met us in a powerful way during the rest of the retreat. Many broken relationships within their church family were restored through God's freedom in their hearts.

There are so many mysteries in this exciting Christian life, but one thing I have learned; His precision timing is always on target! It took me 6 months of unbelievable struggle to finally write that letter. I wanted to make excuses to the school, or possibly water-down the circumstances, but God would accept nothing short of a complete and open confession of my sin. Just prior to the women's retreat, I had made plans to continue my education at the University of Colorado, and had even written to them for an application. What would happen to all of my plans?

I finally wrote to the president of the college with nothing held back, knowing full well that many of the trophies of the past that I held sacred to my heart, could possibly be lost, including the respect of some of the people that I cherished the most. By then, however, I had come full circle to the reality that—**nothing on earth, whether the praise of men or the wealth of nations would be worth the risk of losing fellowship with my Savior!** My Father in heaven had chosen this moment in my life to ask me once again to lay it all on His altar.

Sometimes in our walk with Jesus Christ, we drift into an attitude, or mindset, that we really do not realize has taken root in our heart. God will then prepare a situation to suit the severity of the test. I believe that God had hidden my sin from my memory until all of the pieces were in place, so that I would be able to clearly define what had happened in my heart. I had felt all of those years after college that I had accomplished something extraordinary during my college career, something that the world could never take away from me. I did not realize how I clutched this treasure to my heart, until God asked me if I loved it more than Him. God had now asked me to once again choose between the secret treasure that I harbored as mine. . .and Him. This became one of the most defining moments in my Christian life.

I would never consider my wonderful college experience as worth-less treasure, for it was a gift from God. But, anytime we treasure anything or anyone in our lives as more important than our complete and undivided devotion to God—then it becomes a serious hindrance in our ability to mirror the image of Christ, and we must lay it down.

Philippians 3:7-8 says, *"But what things were gain to me, these I have counted loss for Christ. Yet indeed I also count all things loss for the excellence of the knowledge of Christ Jesus my Lord, for whom I have suffered the loss of all things, and count them as rubbish, that I may gain Christ. . ."*

God does not always require that we write letters confessing past sin, but what He does want in our heart is complete submission to His will. During those 6 months when I fought against His requirement to write to the college, heaven's doors were closed to me. It felt like an impenetrable barrier had slammed shut over my head, and my access to God's throne was closed. Finally, I knelt before Him with a heart of brokenness and knew that nothing else in the entire world was worth being separated from His fellowship. My heart was now refocused on His Lordship in my life and my course had been re-adjusted. I did not even know that self-sufficiency had taken root in my heart, fueled by a secret pride that had been allowed to grow in the shadows. The Bible says, *". . .but as He who called you is holy, you also be holy in all your conduct"* (1 Peter 1:15-16).

Once again, I had learned that the choice to walk with Him, no matter what the cost, is worth more than anything else this life can offer. The issue between my Lord and me was never the sin itself, but my protection of pride that had become an idol of worship lifted up in my heart.

As soon as the letter to the college dropped into the mailbox, my heart swam with the realization that the choice that I had made to write that letter was a milestone in my Christian life. I had been forced to come face to face with the greatest choice a Christian ever has to make. When I chose to give up all that I had clung to, my college degree that had been my trophy of achievement, the praise and honor earned from faculty and staff, and a possible future through continuing education, my heart was set free. God is not against these things. They are all good and honorable goals in our lives, but He is against anything that we cling to and mark "untouchable" by Him. With weeping hearts we vow, "Yes, Lord, everything I have is yours!" But in the secrecy of our closeted hearts, we shroud idols that we dare Him not to touch. All of these things I now saw as "rubbish" (Phil. 3:8-9) compared to the priceless privilege of knowing Jesus.

I received a letter by return mail from the president of the college saying, "Just as God forgives sin, so do we!"

This was a precious bonus of love to my heart. This little covered bridge of brokenness had been prepared by God and planted in my path at this precise time for a very important wake-up call in my life. The many demands for speaking and teaching were beginning to impress me more than I was willing to admit, and God used this incident to jolt me upright.

God was saying, "It's review time! Time to review whose agenda we are presenting here!"

We get so caught up in our own importance and begin to think that God is following us around, like a Social Secretary who runs after us to keep our calendar. I would like to say that this is an exaggeration — but. . .Is it? When this was over, my priorities were straight, and my heart could only praise Him for loving me enough to bring me back to the place of brokenness before His throne.

I would like for you to believe that I learned my lesson so well that this stubborn pride was never able to raise its ugly head in my life again. But the truth is that the sin nature that we have inherited from our father, Adam, never goes away! It must be kept on that cross with Jesus all of our lives. The minute we think we have conquered its ugly nature and leave it unattended, it creeps back into the throne room of our hearts offering to help run things. It can be so winsome and capable, and—yes, so spiritual, that we are sure we can trust its intent! The Bible says, *"The heart is deceitful above all things, And desperately wicked; Who can know it"* (Jer. 17:9)?

We all seem to have an Achilles heel in this area of pride, and the enemy of our soul knows how to find it and how to use it against us. When we take our eyes off Jesus and begin to focus on ourselves and our own plans and resources, he will be quick to use this weakness to cause us to stumble. For one who has suffered with a wounded spirit brought on by the devastating pain of rejection as a child, that Achilles heel seems to present itself as the need to prove myself capable and, in fact, exceptional at whatever task I undertake. This need to prove myself worthy often overshadows the careful watchfulness that is necessary to stay focused on Jesus and His fulfilling life within me.

One of the most familiar examples of brokenness in the Bible is the story of King David and his illicit love affair with Bathsheba (2 Sam. 11). David had remained in Jerusalem while his armies went to war. Perhaps he decided that he needed a vacation. As he walked on his roof, he saw Bathsheba, the wife of Uriah the Hittite, bathing on her roof, and desired her for his own. When Bathsheba became pregnant with David's child, David conspired to find a way to get rid of her husband so that he could take her as his own wife. He arranged for Uriah to be placed on the front lines in the battle against the Ammonites so that he would be killed in battle.

Then, God sent the prophet Nathan to David to confront him with his sin. David immediately confessed his sin and repented before God. God punished David and Bathsheba severely for David's sin and, just as the prophet said, the child of their union did not survive. Jesus says in Luke 12:48, *"For everyone to whom much is given, from him much will be required. . ."*

This verse should be considered by each of us with a great deal of seriousness. We have each received this magnificent gift of grace and salvation at such a great cost, that we must not ever take lightly the responsibility that we have to walk in holiness before those that God brings across our path.

Psalm 51 is David's declaration of Brokenness. This Psalm became a vital reminder to me as I traveled about speaking and sharing God's truth. I always made it a practice to open my Bible on the table before me and read David's words of brokenness just before I stood to share with other women. These words always brought me back to the place at the feet of Jesus to remind me of His great love and mercy toward one such as me. David's words and his heart became my words and my heart before God. They always served to remind me to be careful to stay in this place of brokenness before I dared open my mouth to speak. Verse 17 of this passage reads, *"The sacrifices of God are a broken spirit, A broken and a contrite heart—These, O God, You will not despise"* (Psalm 51:17).

The most painful time of correction in my life came within a few years after my marriage to my husband, Guy. I had suffered through many years of struggle and pain in recent years and was weak and in need of a time of healing. God brought this godly man into my life that became an anchor of strength for my battered heart. Within a few years, we moved to another state, thinking to retire in a lovely southern haven and watch the world go by. I heard someone say recently, "If you are marching in a band and suddenly stop, you will soon find yourself in the tuba section." In other words, you can-not stand still and expect to stay in the same place in your life, especially the Christian life.

Life was so pleasant for me now that I just wanted to rest on all that I had learned about God from the past. Perhaps, like King David, I felt that I needed a vacation from the front lines of battle. The water had been so deep and the river so swift and long, that I succumbed to the temptation to lower my guard. Perhaps I even felt that after such a long battle, God allows His battered children to just observe from the balcony.

This new home was a lovely experience. We found a wonderful church that seemed to be a perfect fit for both of us. The people were warm and out-going, but after a time, I began to miss the exhilarating experience of sharing and teaching God's Word to other women. I was restless and insistent before God to be used by Him, perhaps to prove to myself that God had not set me aside.

There had been so many accusations by the enemy following the years of testing. Would God ever use me again? My heart struggled against the nagging need for proof that this was not true. Before this move, I remember walking and praying about this one day, asking God if He would ever use me again in the lives of women.

As I waited before Him, I seemed to hear an almost audible voice speak to my spirit saying, "Why will you not accept my rest?"

This should have been enough for me, and it was for a time, but I have never been very good at resting. The real problem, however, was that I had begun to focus on my own agenda and my need to prove myself. I began to secretly desire for these women to know who I really was! The trap had been set and I walked headlong into it with my eyes open.

The women's ministry of the church began to plan for a meeting at a local hotel. Their plan was to use available speakers from the church, and I was asked to be one of them. As the day approached, I chose a topic that I had used for women's retreats before—one that had made a strong impact in the lives of the women I had taught. I pulled a chart from my files and carefully went over the notes. I was confident and prepared when my turn came to present this exciting lesson. I even remember opening my Bible out of habit to Psalm 51 and quickly skimming over the powerful words just before leaving for the meeting room. Unfortunately, it was only a rite of passage to me on that particular morning, and I closed my Bible and hurried from the room. After all, I felt I could do this with my eyes closed.

Well, you can probably guess what happened. A series of surprising incidents occurred as I began to share, which left me speechless and baffled before the audience of women in the room. As I remember it, even today, I find it difficult to explain the series of events that unfolded in the room. The only explanation that I am sure of is that God left me completely alone to experience this foolish attempt to carry out His business within my own prideful heart! I had stood before hundreds of women on hundreds of occasions, but never in the many, many years of speaking and teaching have I found myself alone and floundering before an audience of women. I still catch my breath at the painful remembrance of the incident. The sand had washed from beneath me and I found myself struggling for the foundation that I had obviously begun to take for granted. As I drove home that day, I questioned my Father's love that I felt had abandoned me. Even though I knew that I was wrong—like an unrepentant child, I still could not believe that He let me sink like a rock in such shameful quicksand. After all, I was His! Wouldn't He, shouldn't He—protect me from such public humiliation? I must have looked and sounded to Him like a spoiled child, stomping her foot at her father and demanding her rights. I think that this, to me, was a perfect example of God's "Tough Love."

The enemy is always watching and ready to accommodate our foolish and willful insistence to step out ahead of God! I think of the great prophet, Elijah in 1 Kings 18, who boldly challenged the prophets of Baal in the presence of Israel, achieving a great victory in the name of the Lord. Then a few verses later in 1 Kings 19, when threatened by Jezebel, this same man ran for his life (1 Kings 19:3-5).

In 1 Kings 18:30-40, we see the victorious Elijah, the Prophet of God, challenging and even taunting the forces of evil. Six verses later, in 1 Kings 19:1-18, we see Elijah, the man, folding in fear of the angry threats of Jezebel. He is confronted by the word of the Lord in the cave at mount Horeb where he makes excuses for his behavior before the Lord. God then displays His power and presence to Elijah through the wind, the earthquake, the fire—and finally His still, quiet voice. Once again, Elijah makes excuses to God (1 Kings 19:14).

How can a man stand so bold in the power and authority of God one minute, and then turn and run like a coward before the threats of the enemy the next minute? Because after his great victory, he looked down at the waves and the storm, as Peter did when he stepped out of the boat in the storm to walk to Jesus. Elijah, after all, was only a man—but a man empowered by the One Who used him to perform His will. As long as Elijah kept his focus on the One Who spoke with the still small voice, he was as strong and able as God, but when he began to focus on himself, he crumbled before the enemy.

I did not want to include any of this in this chapter, but once again God awakened me in the night with the awareness that there might be others who need to relate to this in their lives. I struggled against it so hard that I began to see my heart's need to, once again, lay it all on God's altar. I have learned that when we work so hard to hide something in our heart, this thing has become a tool of the enemy to stunt our freedom in Christ. A few nights later as my husband and I sat in front of the television together, my heart began to drift into this memory. I began to sob silently as I gave God permission in my heart to show me everything He wanted me to see and use about this experience. It was as if heaven opened to me while God gently played, "This Is Your Life—from My perspective." This had happened quite a few years earlier and had been left on God's altar long ago, but I found that there was still pain around the memory. As I watched God's revelation to me that night, my heart saw from God's viewpoint things that I had still refused to receive. I have said so many times in these writings

195

that even after 50 years of walking with Jesus, I am still amazed at the wonder of His precise timing and His working in my heart. There are times when I am tempted to stop others out of curiosity and ask if God has to deal with them in the same way.

— <u>Four Deadly Steps Away from God</u> —

One of the most amazing things that He showed me was that the notes that I had used with the women that day were about Pride and Brokenness. God had placed in my hand the very solution for my need, but I would not see it! My notes clearly showed the 4 steps that lead us away from God.

The problem in our lives that leads to the first step is **losing our need for God.**

1. This produces an attitude of <u>self-sufficiency</u> **and** <u>pride</u> in our own ability and accomplishments.
2. **Pride** if not checked will then lead to **rebellion**. The Bible says, *"For rebellion is as the sin of witchcraft, and stubbornness is as iniquity and idolatry"* " (1 Sam. 15:23).
3. **Persistent and arrogant** <u>rebellion</u> **and disobedience in our lives will lead to a** <u>deceived heart</u>**, a heart that will no longer be able to "rightly divide the truth"** (2 Timothy 2:15).
4. **A deceived heart is the stepping stone that leads to a life of** <u>perversion</u>. Perversion then sinks its claws into the heart so deeply that the child of God can easily become bound in sin. The account of Saul in I Samuel 13:1-23, and I Samuel 28 is a perfect example of a man that was anointed by God to be king, but pride in his life led him to presume to step out in direct disobedience to God's commands. Saul's persistent rebellion eventually led him to consult the witch of Endor which was very serious sin before God. The Bible says, *"And the person who turns to mediums and familiar spirits, to prostitute himself with them, I will set My face against that person and cut him off from his people"* (Lev. 20:6-7).

All along this treacherous path, God continues to pursue the one who stubbornly insists on going his own way. God, in His loving pursuit, seeks to prevent one of His children from progressing through these deadly steps, and will take desperate measures to bring one of His own back to a heart of brokenness.

— Four Healing Steps Back to God —

There are 4 steps that are necessary for one to be restored to fellowship with God.

1. The **healing** of pride and self-sufficiency in our lives always begins with humility and brokenness.
2. Brokenness and repentance will lead to submission and obedience to God's will.
3. Obedience then, leads us back into the place of revelation and restored fellowship with God.
4. Restored revelation from God will set our feet, once again, on the road to spiritual maturity.

The dangers of unchecked pride in a Christian's life are very deadly—much like an arrogant stroll into a lion's den. The important thing to see, however, is that God does not just stand idly by and watch one of His children plunge headlong into unchecked sin. He will use many strong measures, if necessary, to get one of us to see our sin and repent before Him in brokenness.

All through His Word, God warns the Christian to "WATCH!" Jesus tells us in the Gospel of Matthew, *"Watch and pray, lest you enter into temptation. The spirit indeed is willing, but the flesh is weak"* (Matt. 26:41).

God will show us in many ways that we are slipping into a dangerous place of pride, but we can be very resistant and stubborn to His warnings. Pride acts as a barrier in the Christian's life that stifles spiritual eyesight. Saul's pride led him to enter into the sin of presumption. Because God did not show up when Saul thought He should, Saul presumed to act in God's stead (1 Sam. 13:12-13). So many gifted and anointed preachers and teachers have fallen into the same pit. The temptation to begin to see oneself as *"wise in our own eyes"* (Prov. 3:7) is a dangerous snare that is set and sprung by Satan in his attempt to discredit and nullify the witness and ministry of God's people. We must be very careful and watchful over our tendency to step out and let some swagger of boldness draw even the slightest spotlight away from the throne of God. This is proud individualism and it is deadly in the life of the believer.

There is no greater affront to the deity and majesty of the One Who gave up His throne in glory to redeem and purchase such as me, than to usurp His glory before those He desires to save! **There is no disease more deadly for the Christian than the cancer of pride.** This pride eats away at the heart until it leaves in its place an emptiness that is void of anything or anyone but its own lordship. If left unchecked by repentance, it will strip the Christian spiritually naked before the enemy's gallery of thieves who desire to rob, steal and destroy the child of God. To presume to speak in His name while seeking only personal acclaim is arrogant pride at its worst. I thank God that His great love and mercy toward me will do whatever it takes to bring about my correction. From such a place of brokenness at His feet, one can only look up to observe the tender Father's heart that loves us enough to do whatever it takes to set us back on the right course.

It is a very dangerous thing for the Christian to begin to be impressed with God-given gifts and abilities. We grasp the Holy Spirit's power then take a right turn into arrogance. To do so means that we forfeit the power because power belongs only to God. It will be difficult for the gifted and talented Christian teacher, preacher or leader to have to be reminded that God's ultimate purpose in his or her life is not to lead the world into some magnificent show of Christianity. God's highest purpose for even the greatest in His kingdom is to sit in brokenness and praise at His feet.

The Bible says that *"God resists the proud, but gives grace to the humble"* (James 4:6). We hear these words and know that they are very serious and true, but most of us have a lot of trouble getting this business of "being humble" really settled and working in our spirit. We usually come up with a kind of fake, sickening sweet version of the concept of being humble that serves our own purpose, but bears no resemblance whatsoever to what God means. I have wasted a lot of time dwelling in my own version of humility; a version that is almost always transparent to others in the Christian family. Humility is a work of the cross of Jesus Christ, and can-not be manufactured or counterfeited by you and me! The Apostle Paul gives us the ultimate explanation of humility in his letter to the Philippians,

> *"Let this mind be in you which was also in Christ Jesus, who, being in the form of God, did not consider it robbery to be equal with God, but made Himself of no reputation, taking the form of a bondservant, and coming in the likeness of men. And being found in appearance as a man, He humbled Himself and became obedient to the point of death, even the death of the cross"* (Phil. 2:5-8).

God is the Great Architect of these bridges in our lives and His timing and precision for their appearance is perfect—never a second too soon or a moment too late.

Jesus, knowing that Peter would deny Him, said, *"But I have prayed for you, that your faith should not fail; and when you have returned to Me, strengthen your brethren"* (Luke 22:32). Jesus had told Peter that he would deny Him three times, but He also told him that his heart would return to Him and be stronger than before. It is so painful to remember the times that we fail God, but His love is greater than our failures and those failures often remind our hearts of our desperate love for Him and our need for Him to keep us in a place of brokenness.

There are many other little bridges of brokenness that seem to appear out of nowhere, and just around the bend. Not all of them are painful, but they all leave us breathless with wonder at His great love toward us. These little bridges are like sweet, yet powerful reminders from the Master at just the right time, to keep our focus fixed on Him; a needed reminder that He is the Architect of my life and not me! They always reveal God's overwhelming goodness and His patience and long-suffering toward us. They should cause us to dissolve in praise and amazement before His throne.

I believe that the closest a Christian can come to heaven in this life is to dwell in the place of brokenness. Brokenness is the place of total submission to the will of God and is the opposite of self-sufficiency and self-exaltation. It is complete surrender and obedience to His will and will produce a life of praise and honor to God! This is where we must stay if we are to bring glory to His name, and *"dwell in the secret place of the Most High"* (Psalm 91).

199

— **The Next Step** —

When I first read the wonderful poem "Building the Bridge", by Will Dromgoole, (referenced in the Introduction) the vision of building bridges for others became an exciting quest in my life. This book was written to help guide the way across some of the most difficult bridges that each of us must cross. In an effort to help in these crossings, I have shared experiences from my life and the lives of others. Each bridge bears a unique design, just as each of us is God's unique design prepared for the perfect place in His plan. My prayer is that as each of us travels this magnificent journey, this book will help light the way across some of the deepest chasms and rivers that we each must face.

Yes, there are yet more bridges to cross; perhaps some of them difficult, but we can rest assured by God's promises that each of them will be built just for us and in His perfect time and place. I have learned that our Father's love is vastly beyond the limits of my finite ability to comprehend or define, but I know that it is real and true. He has demonstrated this love to me throughout my life. In the course of this journey, I have felt that my heart could barely contain the love that He seems to delight to pour out on His children, much like a small milk pitcher that tries to hold the content of the ocean. I have learned that the heart of our great God is waiting with plans to change us and mold us into a part of His kingdom so lovely and unique in design that we cannot even imagine the outcome.

This journey, though difficult and hazardous at times, has only served to quicken my heart as I anticipate the next step. I have learned at His knee that I not only can trust Him to design for me "the next bridge," but each bridge that I cross brings me closer to the breathtaking day when I will stand in His presence and behold His face (Rev. 22:4). 1 Corinthians 2:9-10 says, *"But as it is written: 'Eye has not seen, nor ear heard, Nor have entered into the heart of man The things which God has prepared for those who love Him.' But God has revealed them to us through His Spirit. For the Spirit searches all things, yes, the deep things of God."*

The following verse is taken from a poem that I wrote in 2001. These are a few of the words that my heart has heard from the Master builder along this magnificent journey.

"If they call you "peculiar," and laugh when you speak—

Will my love be enough? Will your vision grow weak?
Will you trust me to lead you; to scatter my seed?
Will you patiently seek out the lost, as I lead?
I have shown you my life—the path that I trod.
The road often lonely—the way rough and hard.
The sick have been healed; the lame made to walk.
Now **you** are My hands, My feet, and My heart!"
("If I Give", Sabra Bogart)

The joy of walking in fellowship with my Savior across these exciting bridges can only be trumped by the promise of being with Him for all eternity (John 3:16; John 10:27-30).

About The Author

After the life-changing encounter with Jesus Christ at the age of 15, I attended Montreat College, graduating with a BS degree in Science and Physical Education in 1958.

After graduation, I returned to my mother's home in Jackson Mississippi and began my teaching career in science for 2 yrs. My husband's company transferred us to Kansas City in 1960 where I then taught Physical Education in Bingham Jr. High for a year. In 1966 we were transferred to Philadelphia, PA. However, the climate was too hard on my children's health and the company agreed to move us to Colorado. I loved the adventure of moving from one part of the country to another because it presented many opportunities to teach and speak for women in different communities and states.

My Christian speaking and teaching career began in Kansas City with Christian Women's Clubs and continued with my husband, Glen's business move to Philadelphia and finally to Colorado in the 1960's.

In the spring of 1995 God placed in my heart a dream to share His love and the many testimonies of women in a Christian newsletter to be mailed to women from all walks of life on a quarterly basis. This dream became a reality with the first issue in May of 1995. From there Agape Letters mailing list grew and wonderful testimonies and encouragement entered the homes and mailboxes of women all over the country, and even other countries. This delightful and rewarding ministry continued for 7 years.

In 1986 I met and married my husband, Guy and his first request to me was, "No more exhausting speaking trips." The only logical solution: Write a book. This way, I could cover more ground with God's wonderful message of love, forgiveness and miracle working power than was physically possible for one person.

This book was started in 1993, but had to be put on the shelf for a few years because of Guy's diagnoses of Alzheimers disease in 2004. His care became the most important and consuming part of my life until his death in August of 2011. While losing him was devastating, life with this precious and delightful man of God left me with joys and memories to be enjoyed now and the promise of a wonderful friend for all eternity.

Writing has become the most rewarding, yet consuming thrill of life for me now. I have discovered that when God is "in it," words seem to show up on the pages straight from heaven.

I have a deep love and desire to share God's miracle working truth with women and teens that are searching for life's answers in a broken and seemingly hopeless world. It is my prayer that this book will accomplish that dream while it brings glory and honor to the Name of Jesus Christ. ♥

CPSIA information can be obtained at www.ICGtesting.com
Printed in the USA
LVOW13s1804230514

387073LV00003B/664/P